To Pasqu..
Christmas
Love
Deny

D0382311

THE
Artful
COOK

For Susie, Mums and S.T.

THE
Artful
COOK

SECRETS OF A SHOESTRING GOURMET

RICHARD CAWLEY

Macdonald Orbis

All eggs are size 3
All spoon measures are level
Use only one set of measurements, since imperial and metric
are not exact equivalents

All recipes in Chapters 1—5 serve 6
All recipes in Chapter 6 serve 12

A *Macdonald Orbis* Book

First published in Great Britain in 1988
by Macdonald & Co (Publishers) Ltd
London & Sydney

A Pergamon Press plc company

British Library Cataloguing in Publication Data

Cawley, Richard
    The artful cook: secrets of a shoestring
    gourmet.
    1. Cookery, International
    I. Title
    641.5   TX725.A1
    ISBN 0-356-15215-4

Typeset by Bookworm Typesetting, Manchester
Printed and bound in Italy by New Interlitho SpA

Editor: Gillian Prince
Art Editor: Clive Hayball
Designer: Christopher Branfield
Special Photography: Susanna Price

Macdonald & Co (Publishers) Ltd
Greater London House
Hampstead Road
London NW1 7QX

Contents

INTRODUCTION

A Portrait of the Artist as a Young Man

IT WAS MISS HILDA's port wine jelly at the Coronation Tea which set me off I think on my ever-growing interest in food. Miss Hilda, Miss Dallas and 'poor' Miss Annie were known collectively to all as the Miss Baileys. They lived next door in a large Victorian villa which was identical to ours in every detail – except that the rooms and the curving staircase with its stained glass windows were, of course, all the other way round.

The Miss Baileys were not only wonderfully kind guardian angels, but seemed also to four-year-old eyes to be terribly glamorous and, above all, posh. They drank sherry from small dark green wine glasses during the day, wore make-up and occasionally smoked cigarettes. There was plenty of time for spoiling me as they had a living-in maid called Jean who did most of the cooking and all the housework. On some fine afternoons Jean would take me for a walk on the Town Fields; but more often I would slip around the side of the house and through the little gate in the tall privet hedge which separated our two front gardens, knock on their red front door (ours was only green) and say, as my mother had taught me, 'Is it convenient?'. I never knew what this meant, but it always was, and I would sit in blissful luxury on a high-backed settee which was covered in a dark tapestry of lords and ladies on horseback, my eyes glued to 'Watch with Mother', my small hands clutched tightly around one of the little green glasses full of Lucozade 'wine'.

I started school, we acquired a television of our own, 'poor' Miss Annie died and the Miss Baileys converted their now over-large house into two flats. My world suddenly grew bigger and new chapters opened, but the safe and comfortable centre of my life for many years to come remained the large kitchen

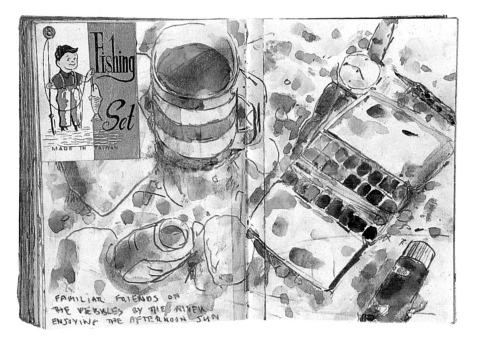

FAMILIAR FRIENDS ON
THE PEBBLES BY THE RIVER
ENJOYING THE AFTERNOON SUN

of our well-loved house. The cooking proper was carried out in a smaller adjoining room called the scullery, which housed the gas cooker, washing machine and stone sink, but I would spend a great part of my time in the kitchen where most of the preparation was carried out.

I can scarcely remember a time when my mind wasn't filled with thoughts of food and art of some kind, and I would watch, fascinated, and daydream as my mother and Great Aunt Nell prepared our daily meals. My mother, round and cheerful in flowered cotton, rolling out the pastry for mouthwatering apple or better still – bilberry pies. My eyes, level with the floury marble slab, watched anxiously for likely offcuts. These I would divide in two. The first half I would fashion with small grubby hands into those hard grey little jam tarts which so many fathers must pretend to enjoy. The remainder of the dough made an excellent substitute for Plasticine, and I would feel myself quite the young sculptor.

Meanwhile Great Aunt Nell would stand by the big scrubbed wooden table which occupied pride of place in the centre of the floor and make bread. A large apron covering her neat lavender crêpe dress, sleeves pulled up over thin strong arms, she pounded away at the dough. After what seemed like an age to me, she would drop it into a huge enamel bowl, cover it with a snowy tea towel and leave it to rise on top of the kitchen range. As I watched and waited for it magically to push up the linen cloth, I daydreamed of joining the ballet or the circus . . .

The scrubbed wooden table not only occupied the centre of the kitchen, but was the centre of our life. Just before mealtimes it would be spread with a seersucker cloth, but on certain memorable afternoons it would be upturned by my ingenious mother. This then became a pirate ship and afforded her an hour on the settee – the kitchen lino with its 1930s geometric patterns was thick with sharks and crocodiles. I remember once overhearing myself being described as 'an imaginative child' and rather liked the sound of it. There was certainly plenty happening around me to feed my hyperactive imagination, kindling a passion for the world of art, to which I had decided I so badly wanted to belong, and at the same time fanning the flames of my ever-growing interest in food.

Piano lessons were my first vision of a world of art beyond my Plasticine and colouring books. It wasn't the lessons themselves: over the many years I spent going to Violet's I never learnt very much about playing the piano. It was the music room with the shelves of books which was a sanctuary, with Violet the high priestess officiating from the altar of her grand piano. My weekly half-hours were precious magical times and I would arrive early and sit and wait poring over the glossy art books which filled the shelves. At seven I was fascinated by Chagal's floating lovers and blue donkeys and Modigliani's thin people with long beautiful faces. Sometimes we would spend most of the lesson just looking at the books and discussing the artists and their pictures – a grey-haired lady and a little boy. Although now I wish I could play the piano which stands against my kitchen wall as I ought to be able, I will always be thankful for that odd friendship and grateful to Violet, her 'piano' lessons and her encouragement – and for teaching me to look.

I knew instinctively that the food we ate at home was good, but I soon began to notice that there were different kinds of food and different ways of eating. Lieutenant-Colonel Foulkes was an American stationed close to our town; when he and his wife moved for a time into the Miss Baileys' flat with their small daughter, the doll-like child and I became friends. It was sufficiently glamorous for me to have neighbours who were American, but to be invited in for a meal was more than I dreamed of: it was all too strange and wonderful. Firstly and inexplicably the meal (which we ate at five o'clock in the afternoon) was called 'supper', and as if that wasn't odd enough, all the curtains were pulled tight and on the polished clothless table there were two burning candles. I felt sure that this was exactly how the Queen must eat. I was given sweet potatoes and other unfamiliar things to eat for the first time. I loved them all, and so it was natural to say 'yes' when offered a Kleenex. I had never heard of such a thing and thought it must be some other exotic thing to eat!

I had another small and equally doll-like friend whose Italian mother would make fresh pasta. It seemed so peculiar that something so like pastry should be cut into long narrow strips and boiled. She served it simply with melted butter, and I liked it even more than the sweet potatoes and Kleenex.

Of us four children, my only sister was the eldest and first to leave the nest, heading for London and college. How I loved it when she came home for the holidays with endless tales of college merriments and fabulous descriptions of the metropolis. One holiday she brought home long spaghetti in a blue packet and cooked it with Bolognese sauce. My father thought the whole thing perfectly ridiculous and it proved for him that what he had always thought about foreigners was right. The rest of us adored it and a twinkle of wanderlust appeared in my mother's eyes. Long spaghetti, however, soon became quite ordinary, for my wonderful sister took me back with her to London for a holiday and introduced me to the bright lights of the big city. It was all a glorious glittering whirl of giant toyshops, theatres and stores like Harrods, but best of all we went to a Chinese restaurant, and at the age of nine, at the end of a perfect day, a patient Chinese waiter taught me how to eat with chopsticks.

The twinkle in my mother's eye grew and she would disappear from time to time to places with exotic-sounding names like Rome, Venice, Capri and Interlaken. My poor long-suffering father, who was more than happy with his conservative diet, was obliged to assimilate such foreign novelties as salami and side salads into his daily victuals.

I inherited not only my mother's passion for foreign travel but her love of discovering something new to eat. 'Race week', or rather the aftermath of it, was almost as much a treat as the extra week's holiday on which we were taken by my father, leaving the house free for 'the gentry' who would arrive with all their trappings to take over our home and avail themselves of my mother's excellent cooking for the duration of 'Leger Week'. These mysterious unseen 'gentry' (who included famous bookmakers, race-horse owners and a French count) always arrived with certain provisions – the residue of which was left as 'perks' for us to enjoy on our return. There might be game birds hanging in rows on hooks in the cellar; the remains of a crate of peaches; some excellent wine; and occasionally something completely novel like yoghurt to be sampled for the first time.

I cannot pretend that the grammar school which I attended from the age of eleven was as bad as Dotheboys Hall, but I hated it as much as if it had been and learnt next to nothing in the five years I was there. More and more, all I wanted was to draw and paint, yet art lessons were considered suitable employment only for 'wets' and halfwits. The personality of the art master unfortunately did little to dispel the myth. Two things happened to me about that time which helped relieve the greyness of those adolescent years. In the first place I took to the stage and escaped as often as possible into the new, exciting and decadent world of amateur theatricals. I was soon addicted to the smell of the greasepaint and the roar of the crowd. I thrived on being 'on stage', but best of all I loved the people – those odd flamboyant creatures with loud affected voices and extravagant gestures, men with beards and women who wore purple stiletto-heeled shoes and sent me on errands to buy long cigarettes in gold packets when most people I knew smoked Players or Woodbines.

The second important event happened when I was still a gauche and gangling eleven-year-old. The next-door flat became vacant once more and was taken by another military family, Squadron-Leader Trotter and his wife. They were not American but from the South of England, though their 'posh' accents seemed just as foreign as if they had been. They also ate from a table with no cloth, and had a daughter. She was called Susan and was also eleven and equally gauche and gangling, so we had a lot in common. The day they moved in her tennis ball came flying repeatedly over the privet hedge on to our lawn. Thus began a lifetime's friendship, not only with another rather lonely eleven-year-old, but with the grown-up Trotters who were to become my second parents and from whom I was to learn so much.

Soon after the tennis ball incident, the Trotter family moved from the Miss

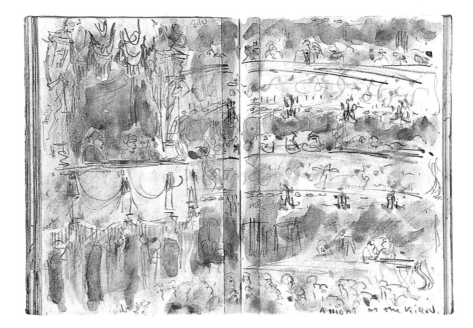

Baileys' flat to a fairytale cottage in a Lincolnshire village, luckily not far away. It was my first taste of country living, and as I didn't want to lose my new-found friends, I spent as much time there as school and my theatrical career would allow. For almost the whole of the long hot summer of '59 we ran wild like two young gypsies, roaming the surrounding countryside until we were tired and hungry, returning to meals which were always wonderful. The cottage had a large kitchen garden on one side and a spacious orchard on the other, and we would feast on asparagus and freshly dug potatoes, broad beans and strawberries and, later, on fresh walnuts from the ancient tree which supported our 'Tarzan rope'. It was in that picturesque stone-flagged kitchen and elegant dining room at Derwent Cottage that I really began to learn about cooking and eating.

From the best of all shoestring cooks, I learnt that a wonderful meal does not have to cost very much. I learnt how to treat vegetables with the proper respect they deserve and how the simplest meal will be doubly enjoyable if beautifully presented and served. I also learnt the pleasures of scouring junk shops for bargains, that all that glitters may not be gold (but can be very effective if used with good taste), and that just because an old box is covered in thick poison-green paint, it doesn't mean that it can't be a sixteenth-century oak chest!

When not exploring the countryside, my inseparable friend and I would spend every waking hour painting and drawing and making things. Those days were long and golden and full of discovery and wonder and my dear friend and I seemed to pass painlessly through the dark tunnel of adolescence without even noticing it.

I could hardly believe that anything which was so exciting and enjoyable could possibly be counted as work when I started at the local art school at the age of sixteen. I think my father at that time also had his doubts on the subject, but resigned himself to the fact that I would not, like him, be an engineer. Probably relieved that I was already too old to take up ballet, he happily sent me two years later to Paris, to learn fashion design. I lived with an aristocratic French family during the year I spent there, and my education in the culinary arts continued over the lengthy and formal evening meals when I learnt that food was a serious matter and that, to the French, nothing short of perfection was acceptable at the dinner table. Spare moments were spent studying life drawing at the Beaux Arts school or haunting the museums and galleries rediscovering so many pictures which were familiar to me from Violet's books.

Over the next four years while at art schools in London I began to put my Derwent Cottage lessons in shoestring cookery into practice. After the usual initial overambitious disasters, I found that I enjoyed cooking food almost more than I loved eating it, but by now I was totally obsessed with the world of fashion. After two glorious years spent in the stimulating fashion school of the Royal College of Art, I slipped into the perfumed and pampered world of haute couture as assistant designer at the thoroughbred house of Bellville Sassoon. The following years were hard work but wonderful and not without a touch of the glamour that we worked so hard to produce for the wealthy and famous women we dressed, rubbing off. The occasional invitation to a reception or a wedding in St James's Palace or the House of Lords made the job even more exciting. In 1984 it seemed, however, the fates had decided in a change of career for me. I won a food competition in a Sunday newspaper and almost overnight I exchanged the world of princesses and silk taffeta for my new life, where most of my time is spent with either a saucepan or a typewriter.

I have somehow managed over the past three years to write three cookbooks and a number of articles on food and travel for various glossy magazines. I have also managed, it seems on looking back, to have been out of the country almost as much as I have been in it. Having my mother's wanderlust, I have always contrived to travel at any given opportunity, and it is often the memory of meals eaten in some far-flung place that inspires me when I am dreaming up a new recipe – whether it be the little chunks of grilled kid accompanied by pink onions, freshly made bread and icy water from the brook flowing under the window of a small restaurant high in the mountains of eastern Turkey; the simple pumpkin curry cooked in a palm-thatched hut on a tiny island in the South China Sea; or the superb nouvelle cuisine lunch which I was fortunate enough to enjoy at Château Rothschild. Meals such as these are firmly imprinted on my memory, but I also have the sketchbooks in which I have always recorded my travels to jog my memory and remind me of other wonderful meals and occasions. I still love to draw and paint and with a miniature box of watercolours, a little plastic bottle of water and a small black sketchbook I can record special moments in a restaurant, on a mountainside or on some sparkling Mediterranean beach. Some of the pages from these little books seem so firmly part of my life that it seemed only natural to slip some in among the recipes and all the other pictures I have so loved making for this book.

While writing for glossy magazines I have been in the fortunate position of occasionally working with rare and costly ingredients, sometimes creating recipes which although delicious have been frankly expensive and need superb shopping facilities to achieve. How much more I enjoyed cooking the easy simple food we ate while camping for a summer by a river high in the Ardèche region of France, where the markets sell only what is local, seasonal and really fresh; or having to produce party food for seventy hungry art students for next to nothing.

I have arranged the recipes in menus throughout the book and these are worked out to give a good balance of textures, flavours, colours and nutritional values. This, however, is just my guideline: you may like to swap the courses around or add something else for hearty appetites, or miss a course, or substitute fresh fruit for a cooked pudding to make a lighter meal.

And now is the time to move on to the rest of the book – the pictures and recipes – and, I hope, for you to share with me some happy memories of times past, and enjoy some memorable meals in the future.

CHAPTER 1

Absolute Beginners

ALTHOUGH THE MENUS IN this chapter have been planned so that they will not be too difficult even for those with almost no experience in the kitchen to produce, more skilled cooks will find them equally interesting, especially when they want to prepare a three-course meal in a very short time. Everything is explained in detail, from ingredients to methods, so that novices will not find the recipes in any way daunting, and will quickly acquire a repertoire of simple kitchen skills.

I have assumed that the majority of 'absolute beginners' are young and will thus probably have fairly hearty appetites. The menus in this chapter, therefore, are composed of quite substantial dishes. For the really hungry the meals can be made even heartier with the addition of bread, potatoes or rice and lots of fresh vegetables. For a lighter repast, simply replace the cooked puddings with fresh fruit.

As you are reading this book I am also presuming that you have an interest in cooking beyond that of merely producing meals as body fuel. Although perfectly adequate meals can be produced with very little equipment, if you intend to develop your interest in cooking, and repertoire in the kitchen, there are a few 'kitchen aids' which might seem like major investments, but which quickly pay for themselves and turn many normally tedious jobs into a pleasure. The one item I would take to my desert island, apart from a sharp knife, would be (assuming that the island had electricity!) my food processor. This indispensible piece of mechanical magic will chop, grate, grind, knead and purée in seconds. I have had mine now for many years, but the more modern versions will also whip, whisk and perform most tasks short of making a cup of tea, pouring a gin and tonic and sewing on a button. If you can't afford one of the more sophisticated machines, there are several very inexpensive liquidizers on the market which, although they will not perform the heavier tasks like kneading dough or mincing meat, will help you to make perfect soups and sauces in seconds. Failing this, buy an inexpensive hand-turned 'Mouli' food mill. Although they take more time and effort than electric machines, they will efficiently purée cooked vegetables for soups and sauces.

Many books recommend long lists of knives and pots and pans and other complicated, expensive pieces of equipment as being essential basics in the kitchen.

These, if all bought at once, would strain the purse strings of even the better-off among us. A bread knife certainly makes the job of cutting bread easier, and a sharp carving knife is a great help when dealing with a large piece of cooked meat, but for most jobs in the kitchen I manage perfectly happily with one medium-sized, plastic-handled serrated knife which doesn't need sharpening. Good saucepans can cost a fortune, so rather than spending money on cheap lightweight ones which will never work very well, search the charity shops, junk markets and boot fairs and you will soon find yourself a collection of good-quality second-hand heavy saucepans which will have much more character and do their job efficiently. Look for bowls, plates and casseroles too. They will be most useful – and you will have had all the fun of finding a second-hand bargain.

Once you have equipped yourself and your kitchen with a few basics, it is time to move on to the recipes. If you are really an 'absolute beginner', cook with a friend: you will learn together, doubling the pleasure in producing something special rather than halving it. Always allow more time than you need, especially if cooking for guests: nothing takes away the pleasure of a special meal more quickly than arriving to find a hot and flustered-looking cook still leafing through a cookery book.

menu 1

FRENCH ONION SOUP

*JUNIPER RABBIT UNDER A LEMON
SUET CRUST*

*COFFEE AND CARDAMOM
BLANCMANGE*

FRENCH ONION SOUP

3 tbsp vegetable oil
3 large onions, peeled and thinly sliced across
1 tbsp sugar
salt and freshly ground black pepper
1.75 litres/3 pt chicken or vegetable stock

1 Heat the oil in a large saucepan and cook the onions in this over a medium heat, stirring occasionally, for 5 minutes: they will have softened and gone transparent-looking. Add the sugar and salt and pepper to taste, and continue to cook, stirring occasionally, for about 5–10 minutes, or until the onions have turned a nice rich brown colour.
2 Add the stock, bring to the boil, turn down the heat to low, cover the pan and allow to simmer gently for 5 minutes. Check for seasoning.
3 Pour into heated bowls and serve with crusty bread. French bread would, of course, be most appropriate – in which case pop it in the oven for a few minutes to warm and crisp before serving.

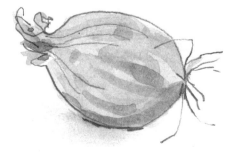

CHICKEN STOCK

1 × 2.25 kg/1 × 5 lb boiling chicken with giblets, cut into 8 pieces
1 onion, washed but with the skin left on, quartered (the skin adds a lovely golden colour to the stock)
2 garlic cloves, peeled but left whole
1 carrot, scrubbed and roughly chopped
1 celery stalk, washed and chopped (optional)
5-cm/2-in strip of finely peeled lemon rind
2 tsp salt
freshly ground black pepper (white if you have it)
1.8 litres/3 pts cold water

1 Place all the ingredients in a very large saucepan and slowly bring to the boil, skimming off any scum as it rises to the surface. Cover the pan tightly and cook over a gentle heat for 2 hours. Alternatively, cook in a slow cooker on low for 8 hours or overnight.
2 Strain the stock through a sieve into a large bowl and discard the solids.
3 Chill the stock for at least 4 hours after it has cooled, and preferably overnight; then remove the fat which will have solidified on the surface. This can be discarded or kept for frying etc. The stock is now ready for use.

notes

Buy strong onions for cooking. Spanish onions or other mild ones are better for eating raw, but expensive for use in cooked dishes, as you have to use more of them to get enough oniony flavour.

A pepper mill is one of the first pieces of kitchen equipment to invest in. After salt, pepper is the most commonly used culinary flavouring. Freshly milled pepper, like most spices, is infinitely superior to the ready-ground type. To be really fussy, a second mill for white pepper prevents little black specks in pale soups and sauces.

Home-made stock is not only cheap and easy to produce, but tastes far better than stock made with commercial stock cubes. Although adequate if you are in a hurry, they always add a distinctive synthetic taste. If you do not have time to make your own stock, wholefood shops sell a vegetable stock in powdered form called 'Swiss Vegetable Bouillon', which is excellent. If you do have time, a basic chicken stock is quick, cheap and easy.

The French, like the English, love animals, but often keep them for the pot rather than as pets. These rabbits and chickens lived in a farmyard in Brittany, where we spent a happy week staying in a *gîte* cooking for ourselves.

JUNIPER RABBIT UNDER A LEMON SUET CRUST

3 tbsp vegetable oil
230 g/8 oz bacon, chopped
455 g/1 lb boneless rabbit (thawed if frozen), cut into bite-sized cubes
seasoned flour
2 large onions, peeled and chopped
8 juniper berries, slightly crushed or chopped
salt and freshly ground black pepper
5-cm/2-in strip of finely peeled lemon rind
juice of ½ lemon
570 ml/1 pt chicken stock (see page 17) or vegetable stock

1 Heat 1 tbsp of the oil in a frying pan and cook the pieces of bacon over a medium heat for about 5 minutes, or until the fat runs. Remove with a slotted spoon (leaving as much fat in the frying pan as possible) and put into a medium-sized, lidded saucepan.
2 Add another 1 tbsp oil to the frying pan. Place the seasoned flour in a small plastic bag and shake the rabbit pieces in this until coated. Shake the excess flour from the meat and fry in the fat over a medium heat until sealed on all sides. (Best to do this in two or three batches, or the pan will be overcrowded.) As the meat is cooked, remove from the frying pan with a slotted spoon and put into the saucepan with the bacon.
3 Add the last tablespoon of oil to the frying pan and fry the onions in this for about 5 minutes over a ▷

notes

Unless you particularly want nice long neat rashers to look good on a breakfast plate, offcuts sold as 'bacon pieces' by grocers and butchers taste just as good and cost a fraction of the price. Look for smoked rather than green bacon if possible; it has a stronger, more interesting bacony flavour. 'Pieces' are often a mixture of smoked and green, but it doesn't really matter, because at such a low price you can add a bit more if necessary.

Seasoned flour is simply flour seasoned with salt and pepper. For this recipe 85 g/3 oz flour, mixed with 1 tsp salt and ½ tsp pepper would be sufficient.

Juniper berries are sold dried and whole and need to be lightly crushed or chopped before adding to food so that their flavour is released. These black, strongly aromatic berries are commonly associated with game and other strongly flavoured meats, and are the main flavouring of gin.

Pastry can be given an appetizing golden glaze by brushing it with an egg yolk mixed with a little milk, or just milk on its own, before putting in the oven.

Suet is the hard fat from around the kidneys of certain animals. Although it is available from butchers in a piece to grate yourself, the ready-grated sort is cheap and much quicker and simpler to use. This comes lightly coated in flour to stop it sticking together and is usually sold in cardboard boxes. Some shops now sell a 'vegetable suet' which is excellent.

◁ medium heat, stirring occasionally, until softened. Tip into the pan with the rabbit and bacon.
4 Add the remaining ingredients, bring to the boil, turn the heat down to low, cover the pan and simmer gently for 1½ hours, or until the rabbit is tender. Check for seasoning and tip into a wide, shallow ovenproof dish. (A medium-sized roasting tin will do if you do not have a dish.)
5 While the rabbit is cooking, make the pastry (see next recipe) and heat the oven to 220°C/425°F/Gas Mark 7.
6 Roll out the pastry to fit exactly over the rabbit mixture, and drop it on top. It does not necessarily have to extend out over the sides and edges of the dish or tin.
7 Bake in the preheated oven for about 30 minutes, or until the top of the pastry is crisp and golden.
8 Divide between six warmed plates, and serve with lots of green vegetables.

LEMON SUET PASTRY

280 g/10 oz self-raising flour
140 g/5 oz shredded suet
generous ½ tsp salt
good twist of black pepper
grated rind of 1 small lemon (if you omit this you have a basic suet crust recipe which can be used for all kinds of pies and steamed puddings, flavoured with herbs or other seasonings as required)
about 6–7 tbsp cold water

1 In a large bowl, mix the flour, suet, salt, pepper and grated lemon rind with a fork. Stir in some of the water and then mix together with your hands to make a dough which holds together enough to roll out, but is not too sticky. (The quantities of water are only a guide; different flours will absorb different quantities of water, so do not add all the water to start with. Only use it all if the dough won't hold together.) This should only take a few seconds, suet pastry being the quickest and easiest to make. It should be made at the last minute and used immediately, unlike most other pastries, which are best chilled for a while before use.

COFFEE AND CARDAMOM BLANCMANGE

300 ml/½ pt milk
8 cardamom pods, split
150 ml/¼ pt water
1 sachet of powdered gelatine
110 g/4 oz sugar
2 heaped tsp instant coffee granules
150 ml/¼ pt single cream

1 Pour the milk into a small saucepan and add the cardamom pods. Bring to the boil, turn the heat as low as possible, cover the pan and simmer for 5 minutes. Turn off the heat and leave to infuse for 30 minutes. Strain into a bowl and discard the cardamom pods.

2 Meanwhile, pour the water into a small pan and sprinkle over the gelatine. Leave for 1 minute, then dissolve over a low heat, stirring, but do not allow to boil. Stir in the sugar and coffee and continue stirring until dissolved.
3 Pour the gelatine mixture into the bowl with the flavoured milk and stir in the cream.
4 Pour into six individual moulds, or one large (600-ml/1-pt) mould; or use small cups or a bowl. Chill for at least 4 hours, or until set.
5 Dip each mould briefly into very hot water and dry the outside with a tea towel: this will loosen the blancmange. Turn out on to one large or six small plates. Delicious on its own, or with cream or soft fruit, or both.

notes

Gelatine is easy to use if you remember a few simple rules. Always add the gelatine to the liquid and never the other way round. Always add it to cold liquid, never hot, and never allow gelatine to come to the boil.

In the Middle Ages
blancmange was a savoury mixture of chicken, rice and almond milk. From Elizabethan times all sorts of sweet puddings made from dairy products became more and more popular and the blancmange was transformed into one such popular dessert, made from almond-flavoured milk set with isinglass. New 'patent' versions appeared in the nineteenth century, which were flavoured milk puddings set with arrowroot or cornflour. The modern synthetically flavoured packet blancmanges bear no resemblance to the home-made version, which makes a simple but sophisticated ending to any meal.

menu 2

PARSNIP AND HAM SOUP

TURKISH LAMB RISSOLES WITH PILAFF
AND GARLIC YOGHURT SAUCE

BLACKBERRY BATTER PUDDING

TWO STRIPED SWEATSHIRTS LUNCHING AT "LE MAS"

While we positively encourage our children to have 'bad taste' in food, taking them to fast food restaurants as treats and constantly supplying them with highly processed snacks like crisps and candy bars, the French begin to educate their children in the art of eating well from a very early age. Instead of being given different food from adults they are encouraged to attune their palates right from the beginning. This young brother and sister were visibly enjoying their lunch in a small restaurant in the Ardèche region of France, and discussing the merits of the various courses with their parents in an appreciative and adult way.

Ham or bacon shanks are meaty knuckles very cheaply available from shops that specialize in cooked meats or slice their own ham and bacon. One large or two small shanks totalling about 1.1 kg/2½ lb will yield about 340 g/12 oz of lean tasty meat which can easily be converted into all kinds of delicious sauces, pies, salads and sandwiches – as well as a good 1.75 litres/3 pt of wonderful savoury stock for soups, sauces, risottos and pilaffs.

Other vegetables and herbs can be added to the ham stock recipe, but this version uses only vegetables available all the year round.

PARSNIP AND HAM SOUP

1 medium onion, peeled and chopped
680 g/1½ lb parsnips, peeled and roughly chopped
1.8 litres/3 pt ham stock
110 g/4 oz ham, finely chopped (meat from stock recipe)
chopped parsley to taste

1 Put the onion, parsnips and stock into a large saucepan, bring to the boil, turn down the heat and simmer, covered, for about 20 minutes, or until the parsnips are really tender.
2 Liquidize the contents of the saucepan and reheat. Check seasoning.
3 Pour into six heated bowls and scatter over the chopped ham and the parsley.

HAM STOCK

1 large (about 1.10-kg/2½-lb) ham shank, or 2 small ones, preferably smoked
1 onion, washed but with skin left on, quartered and stuck with 6 cloves
2 carrots, washed and roughly chopped
1 bay leaf
freshly ground black pepper
a bunch of parsley, or some parsley stalks
1.8 litres/3 pt cold water

1 Place all the ingredients in a large saucepan and slowly bring to the boil, skimming off any scum as it rises to the surface. Cover the pan tightly and cook over a gentle heat for 1½ hours if using a large shank or 1¼ if using 2 small ones.
2 Strain the stock through a sieve into a large bowl and discard the vegetables, herbs and spices. Remove all the skin and fat from the shanks. Cut the meat from the bone and reserve for another use.
3 After it has cooled, chill the stock for at least 4 hours or overnight, then remove the fat which will have solidified on the surface. (This can be discarded or kept for frying etc.) Make the stock up to 1.8 litres/3 pt with water if necessary and check for seasoning: it may not need any extra salt. The stock is now ready for use.

TURKISH LAMB RISSOLES WITH PILAFF

455 g/1 lb minced lamb (your butcher should mince it for you if he doesn't have any already minced)
breadcrumbs made with 5 medium slices of white bread
1 large onion, peeled and grated
4 tbsp finely chopped parsley
½ tsp salt
½ tsp ground cumin
a good twist of freshly ground black pepper
1 egg, lightly beaten
vegetable or olive oil for frying

1 Mix all the ingredients except the oil together in a bowl, then turn out on to a work surface and knead with your hands until really smooth. Roll out into a long sausage shape, then cut this in 30 even sections. (It may be easier to work with half the mixture at a time.) Roll these into little egg-shaped rissoles, then slightly flatten.

2 Fry these in a little oil for 5 minutes each side over a moderate heat, watching that they don't burn. They should be well browned and crisp. Again, you will probably have to fry them in two batches, so keep the first batch warm in a low oven in a covered dish.

3 Divide these between six warmed plates and serve with Pilaff Rice and Garlic Yoghurt Sauce. Just a plain green salad would go well with this.

PILAFF RICE

30 ml/2 tbsp vegetable oil
1 large onion, peeled and chopped
340 g/12 oz long-grain rice (basmati is best), thoroughly washed in a sieve under a running cold-water tap, then dried on a clean tea towel
2 tbsp seedless raisins
1 tbsp pine kernels or other chopped nuts (optional)
1.2 litres/2 pt chicken stock (see page 17) or vegetable stock, or enough to cover the rice in a saucepan by 2.5 cm/1 in

1 Heat the oil in a medium saucepan and cook the onion over a moderate heat, stirring occasionally, for about 5 minutes, or until soft and transparent-looking. Add the rice and continue to cook, stirring constantly, for 5 minutes. Stir in the raisins and nuts if used and pour over enough stock to cover the contents of the pan by 2.5 cm/1 in.

2 Turn up the heat and cook the rice over a full heat, leaving the pan undisturbed. When all the stock has boiled away and the surface of the rice is pitted with little holes (about 10 minutes), turn off the heat and place a tea towel or two layers of kitchen paper over the top of the pan, and then cover it with a lid. Leave for 30 minutes, during which the rice will continue to cook, absorbing its own steam.

3 Fork up the rice, which will now be perfectly cooked with none of the grains sticking together. Check seasoning: the stock will probably have flavoured the rice sufficiently.

GARLIC YOGHURT SAUCE

300 ml/10 fl oz natural yoghurt
3 large cloves garlic, peeled and crushed
salt and freshly ground black pepper
3 tbsp chopped fresh mint (if fresh mint is not available, do not use the dried sort, but substitute parsley)

1 Mix all the ingredients thoroughly together and leave for 30 minutes for the flavours to develop.

notes

Breadcrumbs are best made with slightly stale bread: if your bread is fresh, dry it out for about 10 minutes in a low oven. The job is done most quickly in a liquidizer or food processor; failing this, rub the bread against a grater. If you are feeling really lazy, some bakers sell ready-made breadcrumbs. Never use the brightly coloured yellow sort sold in packets.

Cumin, which can be bought in seed or powdered form, is a member of the parsley family. This spice, with its strong, hot and slightly bitter taste is widely used in the East, Mexico and North Africa.

It always makes me sad to see
the pounds and pounds of
blackberries which rot and
wither on the hedgerows every
year – one of nature's most
plentiful, easily obtained and
delicious free foods. The birds
can't eat them all and we
humans seem to have forgotten
the joys of mornings or
afternoons spent blackberrying.
If you are going to gather a lot
it is better not to collect them in
plastic carriers or bags as they
get squashed under their own
weight. Instead, take wide
baskets or shallow cardboard
boxes lined with plastic –
opened-up plastic carriers are
ideal. Make pies and puddings
and purées and turn any left
over into jams. If you have a
freezer, freeze the fruit in
single layers on open trays,
then turn them into plastic
bags. This way they will stay
separate, and you will be able
to take out just the amount you
need at any time to provide
wonderful treats later in the
year. Blackberries make a
sensational Summer Pudding
in the middle of winter!

BLACKBERRY BATTER PUDDING

110 g/4 oz plain flour
1 egg, separated
300 ml/½ pt milk
butter or flavourless vegetable oil
a pinch of salt
170 g/6 oz blackberries (thawed if frozen)
60 g/2 oz granulated sugar

1 Make a smooth batter with the flour, egg yolk and milk and leave to rest for 30 minutes. Heat the oven to 230°C/450°F/Gas Mark 8.
2 Heavily butter, or brush with flavourless vegetable oil, six large individual Yorkshire pudding tins, measuring approximately 10 cm/ 4 in in diameter (six old saucers would do instead).
3 Whisk the egg white with the pinch of salt until it stands in soft peaks, then fold it into the batter.
4 Divide the fruit between the greased tins (or saucers) and pour over the batter. Sprinkle with the sugar and place immediately near the top of the preheated oven and cook for about 15–20 minutes. The puddings will be brown and risen and beginning to come away from the edges of their tins.
5 Loosen the puddings with a round-ended knife and flip them on to six small warmed plates. Serve on their own, or with whipped cream.

PINES ON THE HILL A
CIPRESSA - NOON

Not all cheap *wine tastes cheap. Don't just go for names you have heard of. Shop in supermarkets: their house brands are often excellent value and have been known to rate highly in blind wine tastings. If you shop in large wine shops, the sales staff are generally knowledgeable and informative. Ask for help in making your selection and don't be afraid to appear ignorant. In fact very few people know much about wine, so it is wise to be guided by those who do. Dry cider or beer can be an excellent alternative to wine with meals, especially with spicy foods. Again, supermarkets often produce their own, every bit as drinkable and much cheaper than high profile brands. A large brown plastic bottle of beer or cider on the table looks anything but elegant, so decant the liquid into an attractive jug and the effect will be quite the reverse.*

In England we must wait until early autumn to gather blackberries, but they are ripe much earlier in the Mediterranean. I picked a bowlful one scorching August afternoon on a flower-strewn hillside in Liguria, where they grew along the sides of a little mule track which zigzagged up between the olive groves.

ABSOLUTE
BEGINNERS

menu 3

CRUDITÉS WITH VINAIGRETTE
DRESSING

SMOKED FISH IN A PUFF
PASTRY PLAIT

CIDER JELLY

CRUDITÉS

**455 g/1 lb small tomatoes, washed
and quartered
455 g/1 lb young carrots, peeled
and coarsely grated
680 g/1½ lb cooked beetroot,
peeled and cut in small dice
2 quantities vinaigrette dressing**

1 Place the three salad ingredients
in separate bowls and pour a third
of the dressing over each one. Mix
well and leave at room temperature
for at least an hour for the flavour to
develop.
2 Either arrange in neat, separate
piles on individual plates, or allow
guests to help themselves from the
bowls. Serve with hot French or
other crusty bread.

VINAIGRETTE DRESSING

**1 tbsp lemon juice
3 tbsp olive oil, or half olive oil and
half vegetable oil
½ tsp sugar
1 clove garlic, peeled and crushed
(optional)
¼ tsp dry English mustard
¼ tsp salt
a twist of freshly ground black
pepper**

1 Place all ingredients in a screw-
topped jar and shake till
amalgamated; or place in a bowl
and whisk. Leave at least an hour
for the flavours to develop before
using. (This recipe can easily be
varied to make a whole range of
exciting dressings: try different oils
such as nut oils; flavoured vinegars,
eg raspberry or tarragon; or add
fresh chopped herbs.)

notes

*Most small French
restaurants offer a selection of
crudités as one of the first
courses on the menu. It can
vary from quite a large and
sophisticated selection of
differently prepared cold,
cooked and raw vegetables to
the most simple and basic trio
of tomatoes, carrots and
beetroot. I often choose this
simplest of starters when eating
in France. When I prepare it at
home it conjures up for me
memories of a favourite little
restaurant in the sunny
courtyard of a farmhouse in
Provence where I have enjoyed
many happy lunchtimes.*

SMOKED FISH IN A PUFF PASTRY PLAIT WITH EGG AND PARSLEY SAUCE

85 g/3 oz butter
1 small onion, peeled and chopped
110 g/4 oz button mushrooms, wiped and sliced
230 g/8 oz cooked rice
salt and freshly ground black pepper
230 g/8 oz smoked haddock
600 ml/1 pt milk
370 g/13 oz packet of frozen puff pastry (thawed)
1 egg mixed with 1 tbsp milk, to glaze
35 g/1½ oz flour
1 hard-boiled egg, peeled and chopped finely
1 tbsp finely chopped parsley

1 Heat the oven to 220°C/425°F/ Gas Mark 7.
2 Melt half the butter in a small saucepan and cook the onion with the mushrooms over a medium heat for about 5 minutes or until softened, stirring occasionally. Mix with the rice and season to taste with salt and pepper.
3 Place the fish and milk in a medium saucepan. Bring to the boil and simmer over low heat for about 5 minutes, or until the fish is cooked and flakes easily. Drain through a sieve and reserve the milk. Flake the fish, discarding the skin and bones.
4 On a floured, cold surface and using a floured rolling pin, roll out the pastry to an even 30-cm/12-in square.
5 Place half the rice mixture down the centre third of the pastry square. Arrange the flaked fish on top, then cover the fish with the remaining rice. Brush the uncovered pastry borders with the egg glaze.
6 Make cuts along each side at right angles to the edges to make a fringe of strips about 1-cm/½-in wide on either side of the filling.
7 Fold the first two strips straight across the filling, one on top of the other. Now, alternately fold over the rest of the side strips, angling them towards the first two, thus making a plait. This is difficult to describe in words but, if you look at my little diagram, you will see just how easy it is.
8 Brush the plait all over with the egg glaze and place on a metal baking tray. Bake in the preheated oven for about 30 minutes, or until the pastry is puffed and golden and the plait is heated right through.
9 Meanwhile you can be making the sauce. Heat the remaining 40 g/1½ oz of butter in a medium saucepan and add the flour. Cook, stirring with a wooden spoon, for 2–3 minutes. Add the reserved milk all at once and bring to the boil, stirring quickly and making sure no lumps form. The sauce will thicken. Turn down the heat to low, add the egg and the parsley and simmer for 5 minutes, stirring occasionally. Season to taste with salt and pepper.
10 To serve, place thick slices of the plait on heated plates with some of the sauce. This dish is quite rich and filling and really needs only to be accompanied by green vegetables such as peas, beans or broccoli or a green salad.

notes

Smoked haddock is a readily available 'cold-smoked' fish. (Cold-smoked foods generally need further cooking, unlike smoked mackerel, for instance, which has been 'hot-smoked' and can be eaten without further preparation.) When buying any kind of smoked fish, whether from your fishmonger or from a supermarket, seek out the label 'without artificial colouring'. Be wary of anything of the particular bright yellow hue only otherwise seen in Teddy Boys' socks.

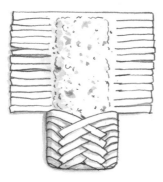

CIDER JELLY

**600 ml/1 pt sweet cider
1 sachet of powdered gelatine**

1 Pour a quarter of the cider into a small saucepan. Sprinkle over the gelatine. Heat gently over a low heat, stirring until all the gelatine has dissolved leaving the liquid quite clear – do not allow to boil.
2 Return the gelatine mixture to the rest of the cider. Pour into six small glasses, six small wetted moulds or one large wetted 600-ml/1-pt mould. Chill for at least 4 hours.
3 To serve, either leave in the glasses or, if using moulds, turn out on to plates. This is done by dipping the mould briefly in hot water, then drying the bottom of the mould and inverting it on to a plate. With a little tap and a shake, the jelly should slip out on to the plate. If not, repeat the hot water process. Serve with cream if liked.

**Slovenia, one of the most beautiful regions of Yugoslavia, is tucked away between Austria and Italy in the Julian Alps. It is perhaps best known for its bees and honey, but in September it seems to be just one huge orchard.
Labrador-coloured cows pick their way through the windfalls and mow the neat meadows around the lakes.**

ABSOLUTE

BEGINNERS

menu 4

MIXED VEGETABLE SALAD
A LA GRECQUE

HERRING SAUSAGES IN
OATMEAL SKINS

ONION AND TOMATO RICE

TREACLE AND LEMON TART

MIXED VEGETABLE SALAD A LA GRECQUE

250 ml/9 fl oz dry white wine
115 ml/4 fl oz water
juice of 2 lemons
100 ml/3½ fl oz olive oil
bay leaf
sprig of parsley (a little bunch of stalks will do)
½ tsp ground coriander
½ tsp freshly ground black pepper
½ tsp fennel seeds
½ tsp salt (or more to your taste)
1 tsp sugar
3 cloves garlic, peeled and roughly chopped
455 g/1 lb carrots, washed and scraped (if using large carrots cut into small sticks about 5 cm × 5 mm/ 2 × ¼ in)
340 g/12 oz small button mushrooms, wiped
455 g/1 lb leeks, trimmed and washed, cut lengthwise into quarters and then into 5-cm/2-in pieces

1 Put the first twelve ingredients into a large, lidded saucepan. Bring to the boil, then cover tightly and simmer over very low heat for 30 minutes.
2 Strain into a bowl. Discard solids and return the liquid to the saucepan with the carrots. Simmer for 5 minutes.
3 Add the mushrooms and leeks and continue to cook over very low heat for 20 minutes, shaking the pan occasionally. The vegetables should now be tender.
4 Tip into a bowl and cool, then chill for at least 1 hour.

5 To serve, divide between six plates and serve with lots of French or other crusty bread to mop up the delicious juices.

HERRING SAUSAGES IN OATMEAL SKINS

900 g/2 lb fresh herring, gutted and heads removed (your fishmonger will do this for you)
breadcrumbs from 2 medium slices of brown bread
1 small onion, peeled and finely chopped
2 cloves garlic, peeled and crushed
2 tsp lemon juice
salt and freshly ground black pepper
seasoned flour, placed in a bowl
1 egg beaten with 2 tbsp water, placed in a bowl
110 g/4 oz porridge oats, in a bowl
vegetable oil for frying

1 Grill fish for 5–7 minutes each side, or until cooked through. Cool.
2 Carefully flake fish, discarding ▷

Coriander seeds – the dried and roasted seeds of the popular green herb of the same name – can be bought whole or ground. They have a delicious flavour reminiscent of oranges, quite unlike the fresh herb.

Fennel seeds are pale and long with a slight aniseed taste. They can be added to a wide range of dishes, both sweet and savoury.

Herrings are underrated fish. Reasonably cheap, readily available and with good flavour, they make an excellent meal simply fried or grilled.

notes

notes

The flavour of olive oil *is inimitable and is delicious for cooking and in salad dressings and mayonnaise. The quality, however, can vary enormously and cheap olive oil can add a strong and unpleasant taste to everything it touches. (Those who claim to dislike the flavour of olive oil have probably only tasted the bad kind.) Better to use a tasteless vegetable oil than an inferior olive oil. Always buy the best quality olive oil you can find: look for labels marked 'extra virgin', which means that the oil is made from the first cold pressing of the olives, and will be the best.*

◁ the skins and removing all bones: this is a little time-consuming and fiddly, but not difficult.

3 Thoroughly mix the fish with the breadcrumbs, onion, garlic and lemon juice and season with salt and pepper. This is best done in a food blender; otherwise knead well with your hands until the mixture is really smooth. It will be quite wet. Divide with a spoon into 24 equal portions.

4 Drop one at a time into the seasoned flour. Though still quite soft, once well coated in flour they are easier to handle. Form each into a little sausage shape by hand and then drop into the egg mixture. Lift out carefully with a fork, allowing any excess egg to drain off before dropping into the oats. Gently roll each sausage over until coated before lifting out on to a plate.

5 Coat the bottom of the frying pan with a little vegetable oil and fry the 'sausages' over a low to medium heat for about 10 minutes, turning occasionally until they are browned on all sides. (You will probably need to cook them in two batches. Keep the first lot warm on a covered plate in a warm oven while you fry the rest.)

6 To serve, place 4 sausages on each of six warmed plates with some Onion and Tomato Rice and a green vegetable.

ONION AND TOMATO RICE

2 tbsp olive or other vegetable oil
2 medium onions, peeled and chopped
350 g/12 oz long-grain white rice
500 g/1 lb tomatoes, washed and roughly chopped
2 tbsp concentrated tomato purée dissolved in 1.2 litres/2 pt of cold water with 1 tsp salt
salt and freshly ground pepper

1 Heat the oil in a medium saucepan and cook the onion over a moderate heat, stirring occasionally, for 5–7 minutes or until soft and transparent. Add the rice and continue to cook, stirring constantly, for 5 minutes. Stir in the chopped tomatoes and add the liquid. It should cover the rice by 2.5 cm/1 in.

2 Turn up the heat and cook the rice furiously, leaving the pan undisturbed. When all the liquid has boiled away and the surface of the rice is pitted with little holes (about 10 minutes), turn off the heat. Place a clean tea towel or two layers of kitchen paper over the top of the saucepan and cover tightly with a lid. Leave for 30 minutes while the rice finishes cooking, absorbing its own steam.

3 Fork up the rice, which will now be perfectly cooked with none of the grains sticking together. Season to taste with pepper and check for salt.

TREACLE AND LEMON TART

The basic shortcrust pastry
230 g/8 oz plain flour
pinch of salt
110 g/4 oz chilled butter, new
margarine or lard, cut into pieces
about 3 tbsp cold water
The filling
4 tbsp golden syrup
4 heaped tbsp white breadcrumbs
finely grated rind of 1 lemon

1 Put the flour and salt into a mixing bowl. Rub in the fat as lightly as possible until the mixture resembles fine breadcrumbs. (If you have had little success in making pastry previously or have very hot hands you should invest in a wonderful pastry-making gadget, which has lots of close parallel blades which 'cut in' the fat in seconds without your having to handle it. All it requires is a short, sharp cutting and twisting action. Alternatively, if you have a food processor the whole pastry-making operation can be achieved in seconds.)
2 Mix in just enough water to make a firm dough: not enough water, and the dough will be crumbly and difficult to roll; too much, and the pastry will be tough when cooked.
3 Heat the oven to 200°C/400°F/ Gas Mark 6.
4 Place the syrup with the breadcrumbs and lemon rind in a small saucepan and heat gently until the syrup becomes runny.
5 Meanwhile, roll out two-thirds of the pastry into a round shape to fit comfortably over an ungreased 25-cm/10-in pie plate. Trim away

any pastry hanging over the edge. Strew the syrup mix over the pastry, but leave a 2.5-cm/1-in border clear. Dampen the border with a little water. Roll the remaining dough into a narrow sausage and arrange in a lattice pattern over the pie, sticking the ends to the dampened border and trimming the edges neatly. (In place of long sausages of pastry you can roll the dough thinly and cut it into narrow strips like flat pasta, then twist the strips slightly before making the lattice. The latter is the traditional trimming.)
6 Bake in the preheated oven, for 30—35 minutes or until the pastry is cooked.
7 Serve either warm or cold; this is quite rich on its own, but sinfully delicious with whipped cream or custard.

Most people relish home-made pastry. Next to suet pastry, this basic shortcrust is the easiest to make. The essential for success is to handle the dough as little as possible. If you have time, leave the dough to chill wrapped in plastic film or in a plastic bag, for 1 hour before using. It will shrink less while cooking if you do this. The shortcrust mix can be made in a food processor in the time it takes to open a packet of the frozen product.

notes

menu 5

*MUSHROOMS IN GARLIC
AND CREAM*

*PASTA WITH BACON
AND CHILLI*

WILD SALAD VINAIGRETTE

BAKED BANANAS

MUSHROOMS IN GARLIC AND CREAM

60 g/2 oz butter
500 g/1 lb button mushrooms, wiped and sliced
3 cloves garlic, peeled and crushed
300 ml/½ pt single cream
2 tbsp finely chopped parsley
salt and freshly ground black pepper

1 Melt the butter in a medium-sized saucepan and add the mushrooms and garlic. Cook, stirring occasionally with a wooden spoon, over a medium heat for 5 minutes.
2 Add the cream and parsley and season to taste with salt and pepper. Continue cooking for 5 minutes, stirring occasionally.
3 Divide between six small warmed plates or little bowls and provide hot crusty bread to mop up the juices.

PASTA WITH BACON AND CHILLI

340 g/12 oz bacon, chopped
1 medium onion, peeled and chopped
1 tbsp olive or vegetable oil
2 small fresh red chillies, deseeded and finely chopped
2 x 387-g/14-oz cans tomatoes, roughly chopped
salt and freshly ground pepper to taste
550 g/1¼ lb dried pasta, any shape

1 Cook the bacon and onion in the oil in a medium-sized pan over a medium heat for 10 minutes, stirring occasionally.
2 Add the chillies and the tomatoes with their juice, and season to taste with salt and pepper. Allow the mixture to simmer for 10 minutes.
3 Meanwhile, cook the pasta in plenty of boiling, salted water until soft but with still a little 'bite' in the centre or, as Italians say, 'al dente'. Cooking time for pasta varies with the brand, so read the instructions on the packet and test a few minutes before the suggested time. Drain.
4 Pour the sauce over the drained pasta to serve. It is not necessary to add parsley to this dish and it certainly does not need Parmesan cheese.

notes

Chilli *is the hot member of the pepper family. It should be used only as a seasoning and treated with the utmost discretion: a little goes a very long way. Choose small red and green peppers and handle with great care, preferably wearing rubber gloves and under running water. Be warned not to get the juice near your eyes or any other sensitive area of skin.*

Tomatoes *are one of the very few products I buy canned. Usually from Italy, they are cheap and have excellent flavour, far superior for cooking to the tasteless fresh tomatoes.*

WILD SALAD VINAIGRETTE

**a colander full of lettuce leaves
a handful of edible wild leaves
(dandelion, ramsons, sorrel, salad
burnet, chickweed etc)
a few sprigs of wild herbs such as
marjoram, basil, or even mint, if
you are lucky enough to find them
one or two wild flowers (gorse
buds, primroses, clover flowers) –
if you find them growing in
abundance
1 quantity of vinaigrette dressing
(see page 29)**

*Not only is this green salad
cheap – the wild ingredients
can be picked for nothing – but
it is great fun to collect. Pick
only from plants that are very
common and plentiful, and (as
with wild mushrooms), always
consult a good book on the
subject before you eat any plant
you are unsure of.*

1 Wash and dry the lettuce leaves.
Wash and dry the wild ingredients
to remove any insect life.
2 Combine all the leaves and
flowers (if used) in a large bowl. At
the last minute, pour over the
dressing and toss thoroughly.

BAKED BANANAS

**12 small or 6 very large ripe but
firm bananas
6 tsp lemon juice
6 tsp clear honey**

1 Heat the oven to 180°C/350°F/
Gas Mark 4.
2 Place the bananas in their skins on
a metal baking sheet and bake for
30 minutes in the preheated oven.
3 Split each banana along the top
and prise open the now blackened
skins a little with two forks. Into each
hot banana drizzle 1 tsp lemon juice
and 1 tsp honey. Place on warmed
plates.

notes

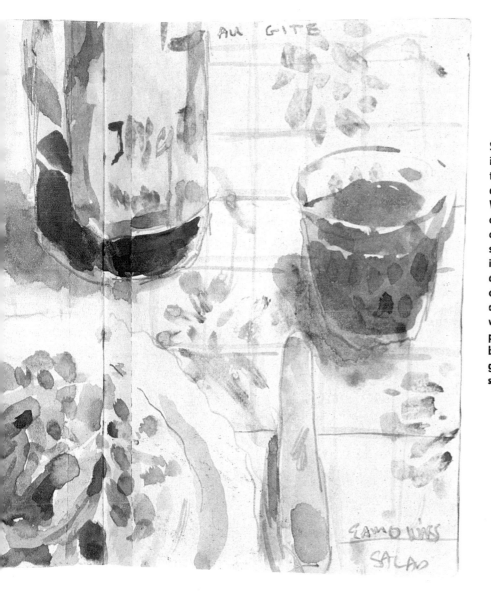

Staying with friends in a *gîte* in Brittany the preparation of the meals was quick and fun as we all made a course each. We always included a salad, often as a first course. Not only was there a wonderful selection of salad ingredients in the local market, but new dandelions, wild sorrel and chickweed grew in profusion along the edges of the lane which ran by the side of our pretty cottage. Croûtons of bread fried in butter and garlic added a delicious savoury crunch to this salad.

CHAPTER 2

DIY Delights

ECONOMY IS NOT THE only advantage of DIY when it comes to food. There is nothing like the feeling of achievement and satisfaction you get when ladling out a steaming bowl of soup made from your own vegetables, bringing a dish of home-made pasta to the table or savouring the wonderful smell of bread baking as it fills the house.

The most useful place to start your DIY for the kitchen is, of course, in the garden. Freshly picked home-grown vegetables taste immeasurably better than any that you can buy: the freshest-looking produce in the shops is probably at least a day old, often much more. If you eat vegetables from your own garden, you can be sure not only that they are fresh, but also that nothing undesirable has been sprayed on them. Those without gardens can plant a 'growbag' or two in a tiny yard, on a sunny step, or even indoors and enjoy the pleasures of eating home-grown ripe juicy tomatoes or really fresh, crisp green beans. Fresh herbs are indispensable to the serious cook and many kinds are quite easy to grow either indoors or out. Even sun-loving basil will grow happily on a bright window-ledge and produce its wonderfully aromatic leaves for a large part of the year.

Another deeply satisfying feeling is to see shelves stacked with jars and bottles of home-made preserves. As a child I dearly loved a book by Alison Uttley called *Little Grey Rabbit's Party*. One particular illustration used to fascinate me. A delicate watercolour picture showed the neat and industrious Little Grey Rabbit standing on tiptoe on a large blue flour bin, reaching up into a tall open cupboard whose shelves were filled with rows of jars, each with a frilly cap. Intriguing hand-written labels described the variously coloured contents of the little pots, and I longed to taste 'Rose', 'Poppy' and 'Lav'.

Home-grown food is undoubtedly cheap, but wild food is free, and there are so many delicious things growing abundantly in our countryside or by the sea that we hardly ever take advantage of. Even city-dwellers can find young nettles, dandelion leaves or chickweed for soups and salads, or elderberries and blackberries for pies, preserves and wines. I gather many pounds of blackberries each autumn from an overgrown cemetery in the middle of the city.

The idea of making certain things at home can seem daunting if you have never tried them before, but the process is usually very quick and simple once you have learned how, and the food always tastes noticeably better than its shop-bought counterpart. Stocks and soups are very speedy to put together and once you acquire the habit of making stock you will hardly ever resort to a cube again. Many of us have tried making yoghurt at home. The first recipe in this chapter is for home-made cheese, which is the next step along from the yoghurt-making exercise. The cheese is as delicious as it is impressive and takes only minutes to make.

Home-made wines and beers can be surprisingly good too, especially when made from wild ingredients. A friend in Gloucestershire makes excellent nettle beer, elderflower champagne and a delicious oak-leaf wine. For occasions when you feel that your hand-labelled bottles are not quite elegant enough, serve the wine from an attractive jug or decanter, as *vin maison* is often served in small French restaurants. A twist of bright fabric or a napkin tied around the neck stops the drips.

We are becoming increasingly aware that some additives commonly found in processed foods can be harmful to our health. DIY cookery is a sure way of knowing what is going into your food and exactly what you are eating.

menu 1

SALAD OF FRIED
HOME-MADE CHEESE

AVOCADO
IN CRUMBED PANCAKES

STEAMED LEEKS
WITH LEMON SAUCE

CHOCOLATE AND ORANGE
DREAM PUDDING

As well as growing your own vegetables, fruit and herbs for your DIY kitchen or gathering 'free' food, fishing can be an excellent way of supplementing your 'wild' food. I'm afraid I have never had very much success, but I do love to watch other people enjoying the sport and admire the patience of people like this solitary man we watched digging for bait on a beach in Brittany.

Lots of national cuisines, particularly those of the Mediterranean and Middle Eastern countries, have their own quick and simple recipes for soft cheeses. This one is almost 'instant' and is very successful. In this recipe it is fried, but it also makes excellent eating just as it is, perhaps drizzled with a little olive oil. You can vary the basic recipe very easily to create your own combinations, adding other herbs, nuts etc.

Avocado pears have now become very popular and plentiful and although they are still not that cheap, they are quite rich. This recipe uses only two avocados for a substantial and delicious main course for six people.

SALAD OF FRIED HOME-MADE CHEESE

2.25 litres/4 pt milk
2 tbsp finely chopped chives, parsley, basil, or other fresh herbs
2 cloves garlic, peeled and chopped
2 tsp salt
150 ml/5 fl oz natural yoghurt
juice of ½ lemon
2 tbsp olive oil
2 bunches watercress, washed and picked over
1 quantity of vinaigrette dressing (see page 29)

1 Bring the milk to just below boiling point in a large saucepan. Remove from the heat and stir in the herbs, garlic and salt, then thoroughly stir in the yoghurt and lemon juice. The milk will immediately begin to separate into curds and whey. Leave for 30 minutes.
2 Line a colander with a piece of cheesecloth or double butter muslin about 50 cm/20 in square and place over a large bowl. Pour in the curdled milk and leave for 1 hour for the whey to drain into the bowl. Reserve the whey for use in the next two recipes.
3 Carefully lift the now solidifying cheese, in the cloth, out of the colander and fold the cloth in half. The cheese in its folded cloth must now be left to drain for 12 hours, after which it will have formed into a long sausage shape. The easiest way is to peg it on a washing line (see illustration). Failing this, pin the edges of the cloth together over a stick and suspend this over a sink.
4 The cheese is now ready to be

eaten as it is or fried. (It will keep for three or four days in the fridge.)
5 To fry, slice the long cheese across into twelve even sections.
6 Heat the oil in a frying pan and fry the cheese slices over a medium heat for about 2–3 minutes each side or until golden brown.
7 Meanwhile toss the watercress in the vinaigrette. Arrange little 'nests' of watercress on six plates, place two slices of fried cheese on each and serve immediately.

AVOCADO IN CRUMBED PANCAKES

115 g/4 oz plain flour
¼ tsp salt
2 eggs
300 ml/½ pt whey or milk
oil or lard for frying pancakes
2 really ripe avocado pears
juice of ½ lemon
6 spring onions, trimmed and finely chopped
2 cloves garlic, peeled and crushed
salt and freshly ground black pepper
2 eggs, beaten with 1 tbsp milk
seasoned flour
crumbs from 6 slices of white bread
vegetable oil for frying

1 Beat together in a bowl the flour, salt, eggs and the whey or milk to make a smooth batter.
2 Make six thin pancakes in a frying pan lightly greased with oil or lard over a medium heat. Reserve.

3 Peel the avocados, remove the stones and roughly mash the flesh with the lemon juice in a bowl. Mix in the onion and garlic and season to taste with salt and pepper.
4 Place a sixth of this mixture across the middle of each pancake, leaving about a quarter clear at either side.
5 Paint around all the edges of the pancakes with a little of the egg/milk mixture and fold up the pancakes to look like Chinese spring rolls.
6 Carefully holding each roll in shape, dip first in flour (shaking off any excess), then in the egg/milk mixture, and finally in the breadcrumbs until well coated.
7 Pour 1 cm/½ in oil into a frying pan and heat over a medium heat. With a fish slice, gently lower the pancake rolls into the hot fat, seam-sides down. Fry until golden brown (about 2 minutes) and turn over and cook on the over side. Drain on kitchen paper.
8 Serve with the Steamed Leeks.

STEAMED LEEKS WITH LEMON SAUCE

6 large leeks, trimmed
50 g/2 oz butter
50 g/2 oz flour
575 ml/1 pt whey or milk
salt and freshly ground black pepper
juice of ½ lemon

1 Quarter each leek lengthways. Wash thoroughly and steam until just tender (about 5 minutes).

2 Meanwhile make the sauce: melt the butter in a small saucepan, add the flour and cook over a medium heat, stirring with a wooden spoon, for 2 minutes. Add the whey or milk and bring to the boil, stirring to remove all lumps. Turn down the heat to low and simmer, stirring occasionally, for 5 minutes. Season with salt and pepper to taste and stir in the lemon juice.
3 Arrange the leeks on warmed plates and pour the sauce over.

CHOCOLATE AND ORANGE DREAM PUDDING

150 g/5 oz butter
250 g/9 oz caster sugar
5 eggs, separated
75 g/2½ oz plain flour
4 tsp cocoa powder
grated rind and juice of 2 oranges
good 300 ml/½ pt milk

1 Heat the oven to 180°C/350°F/Gas Mark 4.
2 Cream the butter and sugar together until pale. Beat in the egg yolks, then stir in the flour sifted with the cocoa powder and the orange rind and juice. Stir in the milk. The mixture may look a little curdled.
3 Whisk the egg whites until stiff but not dry. Fold into the chocolate and orange mixture.
4 Pour into a well-buttered, shallow 1.75 litre/3 pt ovenproof dish. Bake in a bain-marie (see page 62) in the preheated oven for 35–40 minutes, or until the sponge is golden brown and feels firm in the middle.
5 Serve straight from the oven.

notes

Steaming has become a very popular way to cook vegetables. Not only is it one of the healthiest ways, as little of the goodness is leached away into the cooking water, but it can also be very economical on fuel, as a vegetable can be steamed on top of something else which is cooking in a saucepan – potatoes or soup, for instance. The sophisticated new stacking metal steamers on the market are expensive, but lots of very cheap pieces of equipment will do the job just as well. My favourite method of steaming is in a set of cheap Chinese stacking bamboo steamers, where I can steam two or three different things at the same time, one above the other. These are made to sit inside a wok, and are very successful and are easy to use.

menu 2

*FRESH PASTA
WITH TRAPPED PARSLEY
IN A CLEAR CHICKEN BROTH*

*BLACK PUDDING WITH DRIED
FRUITS*

HOT RHUBARB SOUFFLÉ

Pasta is a perfect instant meal. A really tasty sauce can be made quickly and easily in the few minutes it takes the pasta to cook. One of my favourite sauces for pasta is pesto. Its main ingredient is the sun-loving herb basil, which grows in abundance in Mediterranean climates. I have never managed to grow enough at home to make my own pesto, but luckily Italian delicatessens and large supermarkets sell a very good ready-made kind in little jars. I often buy this and it reminds me of some of the delicious meals I have eaten in Italy, like this one in Imperia on the coast of Liguria, in a pleasant sea-front restaurant called 'Ristorante Nizza'. On another occasion, after a shopping expedition, we tried the rival establishment next door and ate another classic pasta dish at 'Il Bigo di Forza'. Relaxing under the stone arches of the long arcades we had two of my favourite Italian dishes: *spaghetti vongole*, full of tiny clams, and *frittura mista dell pesce*, an assortment of seafood quickly fried until crisp and golden on the outside but inside moist, tender and tasting of the sea. Should we really have an appetite for dinner?

notes

Black pudding is a sausage made basically from pigs' blood, with lumps of fat, oatmeal, herbs and spices. How can anything that sounds so disgusting taste so delicious? If you've never tried it, do.

FRESH PASTA WITH TRAPPED PARSLEY IN A CLEAR CHICKEN BROTH

½ quantity of fresh pasta dough (see page 53), not rolled out
about 2 tbsp flat parsley leaves
1.5 litres/2½ pt chicken stock (see page 17)
salt and freshly ground black pepper

1 On a floured work surface, roll out half the pasta dough until it is as thin as possible. Lay half the parsley leaves over half the dough: they should not overlap, and there should be a little space between each leaf. Fold the empty half of the rolled-out dough over the leaves and gently press down. Then roll out again until as thin as possible. The pasta will stick together, with the leaves sandwiched between and faintly showing through. Repeat with the remaining dough.
2 Cut the pasta into 2.5-cm/1-in squares and lay out in a single layer on a flat surface to dry out for about an hour. (They can be kept at this stage for up to 24 hours before being cooked.)
3 In a large saucepan, bring the stock to the boil, check for seasoning and add the pasta. Cook over a medium heat for about 2–3 minutes, or until just tender. (The parsley will now show through a lot more.)
4 Divide the soup and the pasta between six warmed dishes or bowls and serve immediately.

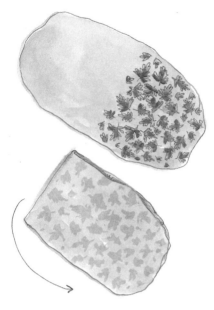

BLACK PUDDING WITH DRIED FRUITS

juice of 1 large orange
2 heaped tsp dry English mustard
150 ml/5 fl oz water
12 prunes
12 dried apricots
2 tbsp raisins
900–1125 g/2–2½ lb black pudding
vegetable oil

1 Mix the orange juice with the dry mustard until there are no lumps. Add the water and pour over the dried fruit in a bowl. Leave to soak, covered, for 12 hours.
2 Tip the contents of the bowl into a medium saucepan and bring to the boil. Simmer on a medium heat for about 15 minutes, or until the fruit is plumped out and tender and the liquid is reduced to just a little sticky syrup.

3 Meanwhile slice the black pudding across into slices about 2.5 cm/1 in thick and fry in a lightly oiled frying pan over a medium heat for about 2–3 minutes each side – do not overcook: the black pudding should be crisp on the outside, but not dry in the middle.

4 Arrange the black pudding and the hot fruit equally on six warmed plates and serve with fresh vegetables, simply steamed or boiled, and rice or potatoes for the really hungry – again simply cooked. A little extra made-up mustard or horseradish sauce is a good idea for those who like it.

HOT RHUBARB SOUFFLÉ

450 g/1 lb young rhubarb (weighed after trimming), washed
2 heaped tbsp granulated sugar, or more, plus extra for dusting soufflé dish
25 g/1 oz butter or margarine
4 eggs, separated
pinch of salt

1 In a medium-sized lidded saucepan, cook the rhubarb with the sugar, but no added liquid, covered, until soft and mushy. The time will depend very much on the rhubarb – from 3–6 minutes, probably. Keep checking, as it breaks down very suddenly and should then be taken from the heat immediately. Now add more sugar if you think you need it, but do not make it too sweet. Allow to cool a little.

2 Grease a 1.5–2-litre/2½-pt straight-sided soufflé dish with the butter. Tip in a little sugar and swirl around to coat the bottom and sides of the dish, then tip out any excess. (This is to help the soufflé slide up the sides of the dish without sticking as it rises.)

3 Place a baking sheet in the middle of the oven and heat to 200°C/400°F/Gas Mark 6.

4 Stir the egg yolks into the still-warm rhubarb and pour into a large bowl.

5 Whisk the egg whites until stiff but not dry with the pinch of salt. Fold a spoonful of this into the rhubarb mixture to slacken it, using a metal spoon and an 'in and over' motion. Keep as much air as possible in the mixture. Working as quickly and gently as possible, now fold in the rest of the beaten egg white.

6 Pour the mixture into the prepared dish and place immediately on the baking tray in the preheated oven and close the door immediately.

7 The soufflé will take about 25 minutes to cook, depending very much on your oven. The cooked soufflé should be quite firm but a little wobbly when pressed on top with a finger. Do not overcook: it is better if the soufflé is a little soft inside rather than dried out.

8 Spoon the soufflé immediately on to warmed plates. I think it is quite delicious enough on its own, although you could serve it with whipped cream or fresh puréed fruit sauce.

Soufflés have an extraordinary mystique attached to them but are not at all difficult to make if you remember certain rules. Fold in the egg whites carefully so as to retain as much air in the mixture as possible – this expands in the heat, causing the soufflé to rise: the more air, the higher and lighter the sofflé. Never open the oven door until you think the soufflé is almost cooked. Serve immediately – the guests wait for a soufflé, never the reverse.

notes

menu 3

OXTAIL IN ITS OWN JELLY

RAVIOLI OF SWEET POTATO AND
BACON

ORANGE AND FENNEL SALAD

EVENING DINERS AT 'LE MAS'

The wine at 'Le Mas', our favourite little restaurant in Provence, was home-made on the farm, as was everything we enjoyed at this charming place. It was also very cheap, and we whiled away many pleasant hours on summer evenings drinking their delicious rosé, gossiping about our fellow diners as we waited for our food.

notes

Most people love pasta dishes, which are not only quick and easy to produce but healthy and nutritious. Look for good-quality dried pasta made with hard wheat or durum flour. Home-made pasta is obviously more time-consuming (though various machines are available for mixing and rolling the dough), but is so delicious that it can be served on its own with just a little butter or olive oil, and perhaps some garlic and a sprinkling of Parmesan.

OXTAIL IN ITS OWN JELLY

**1350 g/3 lb oxtail pieces, trimmed of excess fat
1.1 litre/2 pt cold water
1 × 5-cm/2-in piece of finely pared orange rind
1 large onion, peeled and quartered
1 whole clove garlic, peeled
½ tsp rosemary, fresh or dried
1 bay leaf
2 carrots, scrubbed and roughly chopped
salt and freshly ground black pepper
1 large carrot, scrubbed, diced finely and cooked until tender
ready-made horseradish sauce (optional)
spring onions, cleaned and trimmed (optional)**

1 Place all the ingredients except the diced carrot, horseradish sauce and spring onions in a large lidded saucepan. Bring to the boil and simmer tightly covered over a very low heat for 5 hours.
2 Strain through a colander, catching the liquid in a bowl. When cool, place the bowl of liquid in the fridge for the fat to solidify.
3 Discard all the solids except the meat. While the oxtail is still hot, remove all the meat carefully and discard the bones.
4 Chop the meat very finely and mix with the cooked diced carrot. Divide between six small moulds.
5 When the fat on the stock has solidified, carefully remove every scrap and discard. The stock will have formed a stiff jelly. Melt this in

a small pan and pour equally over the meat in the six moulds and refrigerate for at least 6 hours for the jelly to set. (It can be kept in the refrigerator for up to 48 hours.)
6 To serve, dip each mould briefly in hot water. Dry the bottom of the mould and turn the jelly out on to a chilled plate. Accompany with horseradish sauce and spring onions, if liked.

RAVIOLI OF SWEET POTATO AND BACON

**1 medium-sized sweet potato, weighing about 350 g/12 oz
115 g/4 oz thin bacon rashers, preferably smoked
25 g/1 oz dried apricots, soaked in water for 12 hours, then drained and finely chopped
2 medium spring onions, trimmed and finely chopped
1 heaped tsp dry English mustard
1 tsp salt, plus extra for the sauce
freshly ground black pepper
2 tbsp double cream
½ quantity of fresh pasta dough (see page 53)
1 beaten egg
300 ml/10 fl oz single cream**

1 Heat the oven to 220°C/425°F/ Gas Mark 7. When it is hot, place the sweet potato, in its skin, in the oven and at the same time on another shelf put the bacon, arranged in a single layer on a foil-lined ovenproof plate.
2 Leave the bacon until really crisp but not burned – about 15 minutes.

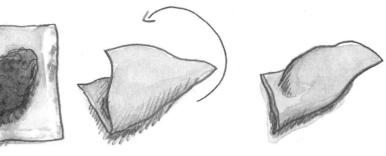

Leave the sweet potato for about another 30 minutes, until cooked: it should feel really soft when squeezed, like a baked ordinary potato.

3 Drain the fat from the bacon and reserve for another use. Then crumble the rashers finely.

4 Scoop the flesh of the cooked potato into a bowl and discard the skin. Mash the flesh and mix well with the crumbled bacon, the chopped apricots and onions, the mustard, salt and pepper. Moisten with cream.

5 Roll out the pasta dough as thinly as possible, working in two halves to make it more manageable, and cut into 5-cm/2-in squares. You should have about 48, but a few more or less doesn't really matter.

6 Place about half a teaspoon of the sweet potato mixture into the centre of each pasta square. Do not put too much, or you will have difficulty folding over the dough (next step): try a few first, until you have the quantity right.

7 Brush two adjoining sides of each square very lightly with beaten egg and fold these over, sticking them to the other two sides, to form little triangular cushions. This is much easier and quicker than it sounds, and once you have made a few you

will soon get the knack. They can be cooked immediately or kept in the fridge for up to 48 hours.

8 Put a large pan of salted water on to boil while you make the sauce. For this simply heat the single cream in a small saucepan and season to taste with salt and pepper.

9 When the water comes to the boil, tip in the ravioli and cook for about 2–3 minutes. Then drain and return to the pan.

10 Pour the hot cream on to the ravioli and toss gently until all are coated, then divide between six hot bowls or dishes.

ORANGE AND FENNEL SALAD

3 large oranges, peeled and thinly sliced across
675 g/1½ lb fennel, trimmed and thinly sliced across
1 quantity of vinaigrette (see page 29), with garlic if liked

1 In an attractive bowl, mix the orange and fennel slices with the dressing and leave at room temperature for at least 1 hour before serving for the flavours to develop.

notes

Pasta is simply a mixture of eggs and flour, and can be made using nothing more than your hands and a large rolling pin. Mix 3 eggs with 300 g/10½ oz flour (durum flour bought from an Italian shop is best, but strong white and even ordinary plain white produce excellent results) to make a stiff dough, then knead on a floured work surface for 10 minutes.

To roll out, divide the dough into four pieces and roll each out as thinly as you possibly can. Unless you are making stuffed pasta such as ravioli (when you don't allow the dough to dry), hang the dough over the washing line (or a clean broom handle or bamboo pole balanced on the backs of two chairs) to dry for 1 hour. To make noodles such as tagliatelle, roll each dried sheet of dough into a cylinder, cut across at 1-cm/½-in intervals, and then separate the strips – which are now ready to cook.

menu 4

FIVE ONION SOUP

HAM AND SWEETCORN PANCAKE PIE

*'TAGLIATELLE' OF CARROTS AND
COURGETTES*

GINGER JELLY

The pig was often the most pampered member of cottage households in the nineteenth century. He had to be well looked after and fattened up for the winter when he would be slaughtered. The resulting joints would be cured and hung in the chimney piece to last all the winter. For many households tiny morsels of this bacon would be the only meat eaten to relieve the monotony of a diet which in winter months consisted mainly of potatoes and cabbage.

notes

Onions are so versatile. The many members of the onion family all taste different from one another, and (like potatoes) each varies according to how – or even whether – it is cooked. This soup recipe uses five types: as well as ordinary onions, it contains mild-tasting leeks and pungent garlic; it is finished with the sharp taste of spring onions and garnished with bright green chives.

FIVE ONION SOUP

1.5 litres/2½ pt chicken stock (see page 17), or vegetable stock
2 large leeks, trimmed, roughly chopped and thoroughly washed
2 large onions, peeled and roughly chopped
2 cloves garlic, peeled and crushed
300 ml/10 fl oz milk
salt and freshly ground black pepper
6 spring onions, trimmed and finely sliced across, including the green part
2 tbsp chopped chives

1 Put the stock, leeks, onions and garlic into a large lidded saucepan. Bring to the boil. Turn down the heat and simmer, covered, for about 20 minutes or until the vegetables are soft.
2 Liquidize the contents of the pan and return to the pan with the milk; season if necessary with salt and pepper. Bring back to the boil and add the chopped spring onions. Simmer for 2 minutes.
3 Pour into six warmed dishes or bowls and sprinkle with chopped chives.

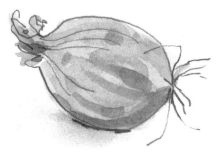

HAM AND SWEETCORN PANCAKE PIE

2 small ham shanks or 1 large one (total weight about 1.10 kg/2½ lb)
1 large onion, peeled and quartered and stuck with 8 whole cloves
sprig of parsley or a few parsley stalks
pinch of dried thyme, or sprig of fresh if available
1 bay leaf
8 whole black peppercorns
2 litres/3½ pt water
The pancakes
115 g/4 oz plain flour
2 eggs
¼ tsp salt
300 ml/½ pt milk
oil for frying
The sauce
50 g/2 oz butter
50 g/2 oz flour
2 tsp dry English mustard
575 ml/1 pt milk
salt and freshly ground black pepper
3 spring onions, trimmed and finely chopped
1 tbsp finely chopped parsley
170 g/6 oz sweetcorn kernels (drained if canned, thawed if frozen)
45 g/1½ oz butter
breadcrumbs from 2 medium slices of white bread

1 First put the ham shanks, onion quarters stuck with cloves, parsley, thyme, bay leaf, peppercorns and water in a large lidded saucepan and bring to the boil, skimming off with a slotted spoon and discarding any scum as it rises to the surface. Cover and simmer over a low heat for 1½ hours for two small shanks and 2 hours for one large one.

2 Remove the ham shanks, cut off the skin and discard. Then cut off all the meat, discarding any fat. This is most easily done while the meat is still hot. Cut into bite-size pieces and set aside.

3 Strain the stock and discard the solids. A little liquid will have evaporated, but you should be left with about 1.75 litres/3 pt. It may not need any salt, as the meat is salty. Refrigerate this stock and keep to make risottos or soups (such as the 'London Particular' pea soup). Now make the pancakes.

4 Mix together the flour, eggs, salt and milk to make a smooth batter, and allow to rest for 30–60 minutes.

5 Heat a medium-sized frying pan, brush with a little oil, and make six pancakes over a medium heat, turning each one over when the underside is golden brown. Stack on a plate. (Depending on the size of pan and the thickness of the pancakes, you may get more than six pancakes from this batter. It does not matter: the next steps will remain the same even if you use more pancakes.) Heat the oven to 200°C/400°F/Gas Mark 6.

6 For the sauce: melt the butter in a medium saucepan and add the flour and mustard. Cook, stirring constantly, over a medium heat for 2–3 minutes. Add the milk and stir well to make sure there are no lumps. When the sauce comes to the boil, turn down as low as possible and simmer for 5 minutes, stirring occasionally. Remove from

the heat and stir in the reserved ham, onions, parsley and corn.

7 Using half the butter, generously grease a straight-sided round ovenproof dish or solid-bottomed cake tin – a soufflé dish is ideal. (The circumference should be as near the same as that of the frying pan as possible, so that the pancakes will fit in snugly.)

8 Tip the breadcrumbs into the dish or tin and swizzle round to coat the bottom and sides. Tip out the remaining breadcrumbs and reserve.

9 Now drop the pancakes into the mould, one by one, with a layer of the ham mixture between each, until all the pancakes and all the ham mixture are used up. Start and finish with a pancake. Sprinkle on the reserved breadcrumbs and remaining butter, cut into tiny pieces.

10 Cover with a piece of kitchen foil and bake in the centre of the preheated oven for 20 minutes, removing the foil for the last 5 minutes to brown the top. The 'pie' should be hot and slightly bubbling around the edges, with the top crisp and brown: if not, return to the oven for another 5 minutes. Leave at room temperature for 10 minutes before serving.

11 This 'pie' can be turned out on to a serving platter if you are careful and wish to serve it at the table. If you are nervous it can be sliced and served from the dish like lasagne, but you will not have such neat slices. This is a filling dish and is probably best served only with fresh green vegetables, like the following recipe.

notes

Parsley *is perhaps the most universally popular herb, although sometimes over-used. It has a distinctive flavour and it is a mistake to add it in cooking or sprinkle it over food indiscriminately. If you can find the flat-leafed Continental variety, very similar in appearance to fresh coriander, it has a better flavour and texture than the more common curly variety. I buy a big bunch. It keeps at least a week in a glass of water on my window ledge and adds a welcome splash of colour.*

My Gloucestershire friend, who makes so many wonderful preserves, pickles, jams and country wines, often sets a little arrangement of jams and jellies in a deeply recessed window of her old Cotswold stone house, just for the pleasure of seeing the sunlight shining through the glass pots and making the preserves glow like jewels.

'TAGLIATELLE' OF CARROTS AND COURGETTES

225 g/8 oz young carrots, scrubbed and trimmed
225 g/8 oz small courgettes, washed and dried
salt and freshly ground black pepper
finely chopped parsley (optional)

1 Slice the vegetables into long thin ribbons with a vegetable peeler.
2 Arrange the vegetable strips loosely in the top half of a steamer and sprinkle lightly with salt. Steam over boiling water for only 2–3 minutes. The vegetables should be hot but still a little crisp.
3 Serve sprinkled with a little pepper and chopped parsley if you wish.

GINGER JELLY

850 ml/1½ pt fizzy dry ginger ale
1½ sachets of powdered gelatine

1 Set aside 50 ml/2 fl oz of the ginger ale. Place the rest in its bottle in the fridge and leave for several hours until really cold. At the same time chill six medium glasses in the fridge.
2 Melt the gelatine in the reserved ginger ale and allow to cool until just on the point of thickening. Then, working very quickly, mix the gelatine mixture with the cold ginger ale, pour immediately into the chilled glasses and return to the fridge. Leave for at least 4 hours before serving.

menu 5

NETTLE SOUP

HOT TERRINE OF LAMB
IN AN AUBERGINE COAT

GARLIC CREAM SAUCE

ALMOND CHIVE RICE

PEAR UPSIDE-DOWN TART

NETTLE SOUP

1 tbsp vegetable oil
1 large onion, peeled and chopped
225 g/8 oz nettle tops, washed and drained
2 cloves garlic, peeled and crushed
1.1 litre/2 pt chicken stock (see page 17) or vegetable stock
300 ml/½ pt milk
salt and freshly ground black pepper

1 Heat the oil in a large lidded saucepan and cook the onion over a medium heat, stirring occasionally, until soft and transparent.
2 Add the nettles, garlic and stock and bring to the boil, cover the pan and simmer over a gentle heat for 15 minutes.
3 Liquidize the soup and return to the pan. Stir in the milk and reheat. Season to taste with salt and pepper and serve in heated bowls or dishes.

HOT TERRINE OF LAMB IN AN AUBERGINE COAT

1 large or 2 small aubergines, weighing about 500 g/1 lb
salt
2 tbsp olive oil
1 medium onion, peeled and chopped
1 stick of celery, cleaned, trimmed and finely chopped
550 g/1¼ lb minced raw lamb
1 tsp rosemary, finely chopped
finely grated rind of ½ lemon
2 cloves garlic, peeled and crushed
1 heaped tbsp concentrated tomato purée
1 egg, lightly beaten
2 tbsp double cream
salt and freshly ground black pepper

1 Slice the aubergine into slices about 5 mm/¼ in thick. Sprinkle on both sides with salt, place in a colander over the sink and leave for 30 minutes. The salt will draw out the bitter juices. Rinse off the salt and juices under cold water and pat the slices dry with kitchen paper. Meanwhile, heat the oven to 220°C/425°F/Gas Mark 7.
2 Using a tablespoon of the oil, brush a large baking sheet and lay the aubergine slices on it in one layer. Then brush a little oil over the top of the slices. Bake in the preheated oven for 15 minutes. Remove and allow to cool. Reset the oven temperature to 200°C/400°F/Gas Mark 6.
3 Meanwhile, heat the remaining ▷

notes

I love cooking nettles: it seems such sweet revenge for all those horrid stings on bare childish legs to eat and enjoy the offending spiteful little leaves. If you have never tried them, you will be pleasantly surprised: nettles are not only free and plentiful (often rather too much so!), but delicious, tasting like spinach. Use only the small top leaves from young nettles, picking them with gloves on, and wash well in plenty of salted cold water to remove any unwanted small animals. Stinging nettles have much the best flavour (all the sting disappears when they are cooked) but dead-nettles have prettier flowers of red, yellow or – more commonly – white. These last have the romantic name of archangels, and I like to put a vase of them on the table when serving this soup.

notes

A bain-marie *is a large shallow pan (perhaps a roasting tin) containing hot water, in which stands a smaller dish of food (such as custard) that needs gentle cooking via indirect heat.*

◁ 1 tbsp oil in a small saucepan and cook the onion and celery over a medium heat, stirring occasionally, till softened – about 10 minutes.

4 Line the bottom and sides of a lightly oiled 850-ml/1½-pt loaf tin with the aubergine slices, overlapping slightly. Reserve some for the top.

5 Mix the lamb with the cooked onion and celery, the rosemary, lemon rind, garlic, tomato purée, egg and cream, and season with salt and pepper.

6 Press the meat mixture well into the lined loaf tin and cover the top with the remaining aubergine slices. Cover tightly with kitchen foil, place in a bain-marie and cook in the preheated oven for 1 hour. Remove from the oven, turn out on to a flat surface and cut into six even slices.

7 Arrange a slice of the terrine on each of the six hot plates and spoon over a little Garlic Cream Sauce. Serve with Almond Chive Rice and a green vegetable.

GARLIC CREAM SAUCE

1 whole head of garlic, separated into cloves and peeled
2 tbsp single cream
salt and freshly ground black pepper

1 Place all the cloves of garlic in a small saucepan, cover with cold water, bring to the boil and simmer over a low heat for 5 minutes. Drain.

2 Repeat stage 1 twice more: the garlic will have been cooked in three lots of water for 15 minutes.

3 Mash the cooked garlic and stir in the cream. Season to taste with salt and pepper.

ALMOND CHIVE RICE

2 tbsp vegetable oil
1 large onion, peeled and chopped
350 g/12 oz long-grain rice, thoroughly washed in a sieve under a running cold-water tap, then dried on a clean tea towel
about 1.1 litres/2 pt of cold water
salt and freshly ground black pepper
50 g/2 oz slivered almonds, toasted until golden brown
2 tbsp finely chopped chives

1 Heat the oil in a medium saucepan and cook the onion over a moderate heat, stirring occasionally, for about 5 minutes, or until soft and transparent-looking. Add the rice and continue to cook, stirring constantly, for 5 minutes. Pour over enough water to cover the rice by 2.5 cm/1 in.

2 Turn up the heat and cook the rice over a full heat, leaving the pan undisturbed. When all the water has boiled away and the surface of the rice is pitted with little holes (about 10 minutes), turn off the heat and place a tea towel or two layers of kitchen paper over the top of the pan and then cover it with the lid. Leave for 30 minutes, during which the rice will continue to cook, absorbing its own steam.

3 Fork up the rice, which will now be perfectly cooked with none of the grains sticking together. Season to taste with salt and pepper. Stir in the almonds and chives.

PEAR UPSIDE-DOWN TART

675 g/1½ lb dessert pears
juice of ½ lemon
115 g/4 oz unsalted butter
115 g/4 oz granulated sugar
1 tbsp brandy (optional)
½ quantity of puff pastry

1 Peel and core the pears; quarter it large, cut into halves if small. Toss in the lemon juice, and reserve.
2 Melt the butter in a 25 cm/10-in round flameproof dish or flan tin (I use a small paella pan). Cool and sprinkle over the sugar in an even layer. Then arrange the pear quarters (or halves) in a single layer in the pan, flat sides up. Sprinkle over the brandy, if used.
3 On a lightly floured surface roll out the pastry to a good 25-cm/10-in circle. Lay it over the pears in the pan and chill for 30 minutes to 1 hour. Meanwhile, heat the oven to 220°C/425°F/Gas Mark 7.
4 Put the dish or tin over a direct medium—full heat for 15 minutes. The butter and sugar will caramelize and the pears be half-cooked.
5 Bake the tart in the preheated oven for 20 minutes, or until the pastry is crisp and golden.
6 Invert the tart on to a serving dish, slice in wedges and serve hot or at room temperature.

PUFF PASTRY

225 g/8 oz plain flour
½ tsp salt
225 g/8 oz cold unsalted butter
100 ml/4 fl oz ice-cold water

1 Place the flour and salt in a mixing bowl and rub in 25 g/1 oz of the butter. Add the water and mix with a fork, then quickly knead with cold hands (run them under the cold tap if they are hot) to form a soft dough. Wrap the dough in plastic film and chill for 10 minutes.
2 On a well-floured work surface, gently shape with a well-floured rolling pin the remaining cold butter to a 10-cm/4-in square.
3 On a floured surface roll out the chilled dough to a square measuring 23 cm/9 in.
4 Place the butter square diagonally on the dough square and then fold the corners of the dough over to the centre like an envelope, slightly overlapping, and enclosing the butter completely. Press lightly with the rolling pin to seal the edges.
5 Lay the pastry seam-side down and quickly roll out to a rectangle two-and-a-half times its width. Fold the bottom third up over the centre and the top third down over it, and press down gently with a rolling pin to seal the three layers. This rolling and folding is called a 'turn'. Rotate the folded pastry through 90°. Repeat the rolling and folding to complete the second turn. Cover in plastic film. Chill for 20 minutes.
6 Give the pastry two more turns, chill for another 20 minutes, then give two final turns. The puff pastry is then ready to roll out and use.

notes

Bought puff pastry *produces very good results and I always used to think that it wasn't worth making my own — that is, until I learnt how easy it is. Once you have the knack, it doesn't take very long at all, even allowing for the pastry to rest in the fridge between 'turns'. The important thing is to use really good unsalted butter: using anything else is false economy, and since it goes such a long way, it is not expensive anyway. I still use bought puff pastry for lots of dishes, but sometimes the special flavour of the real home-made version makes all the difference, as in Pear Upside-down Tart.*

Simple Pleasures

Inside Freddy Ashley's home all was peace and quiet and spotless purity. The walls were freshly whitewashed, the table and board floor were scrubbed to a pale straw colour, the beautifully polished grate glowed crimson, for the oven was being heated, and placed half way over the table was a snowy cloth with a paste-board and rolling-pin upon it. Freddy was helping his mother make biscuits, cutting the pastry she had rolled into shapes with a little tin cutter. Their two faces, both so plain and yet so pleasant, were close together over the paste-board and their two voices as they bade Laura come in and sit by the fire sounded like angels' voices after the tumult outside.
From *Lark Rise to Candleford* by Flora Thompson, Oxford University Press 1945

FLORA THOMPSON'S DESCRIPTION OF the beautiful quiet calm of the Ashleys' kitchen in *Lark Rise to Candleford* seems like a haven of peace into which I should love to escape from the hurly-burly world we live in almost a century later. How pleasant it would be to be invited, like Laura, to 'come in and sit by the fire'. The Ashleys, like everyone else in the village of Lark Rise, were very poor and although no-one would now care to return to an age of such poverty and hardship, in some ways they were much better off than we are now. In our computer-dominated age, unfortunately, we seem almost to have lost the capacity to enjoy the truly simple but essential pleasures of life. The ancient ritual of sharing a meal with close family or friends is surely one of the most pleasant ways to relax, and with this in mind the menus in this chapter are intended to give pleasure rather than to impress. Some of the meals are composed of a very small selection of basic ingredients simply combined and prepared. Others are based on old-fashioned, much-loved and comforting classics, like boiled salt-beef and pease pudding or nursery favourites like Queen of Puddings.

Now that so much of the food we eat comes to us so carefully manicured and glossily packaged it is easy to lose track of where it comes from. It is for this reason that I have begun this chapter with a quick and easy recipe for delicious home-made bread. Simple and nourishing, bread has been one of the world's essential staple foods in one form or another since ancient times. Although it would be rather impracticable for most of us to adopt a total 'back-to-nature' life style, the comfortable pleasure of making bread never grows less, and with the help of modern technology in the shape of 'fast-action' yeast, it is easy to fit this task into our busy lives.

There is a tendency today to be over-fussy when preparing food but the simplest things are always best – provided you have shopped for the freshest and best ingredients. One of the nicest meals of all for me is a perfectly plain omelette with a simple green salad in a good dressing and some fresh crusty bread. With a glass of cold white wine it becomes a feast. A good omelette is ridiculously easy to make. For two people, break three or four eggs into a bowl and add a teaspoon of cold water for each egg, a little salt and a good grind of black pepper. Mix together with a fork. Melt a good knob of butter (not margarine) in a medium-sized frying pan over a high heat. As soon as the butter is really hot and sizzling, but before it turns brown, tip in the egg mixture and swizzle it around to cover the bottom of the pan. As the egg begins to set, keep lifting up the edges with a knife so that the uncooked egg runs underneath and comes into contact with the hot pan. As soon as the omelette is almost set, but not dry, flip it in half and slide it on to a hot plate. Once folded it will continue to cook for a few seconds in its own heat.

menu 1

HOME-MADE BREAD

BRAISED CHICORY

*ROASTED SHOULDER OF LAMB WITH
GARLIC, ROSEMARY AND LEMON*

POTATOES DAUPHINOISE

*CELERY WITH ALMOND CHEESE AND
MANGO CHUTNEY*

HOME-MADE BREAD

675 g/1½ lb unbleached white flour
1½ tsp salt
15 g/½ oz butter or lard
1 sachet of 'fast-action' yeast
400 ml/14 fl oz hand-hot water

1 Place the flour in a large bowl with the salt and rub in the fat as you would for making pastry. Mix in the yeast with a fork and then stir in the hot water, bringing the mixture together to form a ball of dough.
2 Now you must knead the dough for at least 10 minutes: do not skimp on the kneading time. Place the ball of dough on a floured surface, and holding the ball of dough at one edge with one hand, stretch it away from you with the ball of the other hand, using a sort of bashing, pushing and stretching movement. Fold it in half and give the dough a quarter turn on the work surface, then repeat the process. This is what you must continue to do for 10–15 minutes: it is quite hard work, but wonderfully therapeutic. It is also a good way to get rid of any built-up tension. ▷

'Fast-action' yeast makes many kinds of baking quicker and easier: it is mixed with the dry ingredients and then the warm liquid is added. The dough only needs to rise once before baking – unlike the other kinds of yeast, when it needs two risings.

◁ **3** Form the dough into an even ball and place on a floured board. Sprinkle the top well with flour and cover with a lightweight clean cloth which you have also sprinkled lightly with flour. Leave in a warm place, (not too warm – just an average kitchen will do) and leave to rise until doubled in size. It is better to leave the dough to rise slowly rather than to force it in an airing cupboard for instance. It also usually takes rather longer to rise than it will tell you on the yeast packet. The time will depend on the temperature, humidity etc, but allow 2–3 hours.
4 Meanwhile heat the oven to 230°C/450°F/Gas Mark 8. Place a metal baking tray in the oven on a centre shelf, and a small heatproof bowl of boiling water on the floor of the oven to provide humidity.
5 When the oven is really hot, sprinkle the risen dough with a little more flour and make two quick slashes across the top with a sharp knife to form a cross. This will release any 'tensions' in the dough as it cooks and will help to produce a nice evenly shaped loaf. It also gives the bread a nice homely look.
6 With a quick flicking motion, tip the loaf on to the hot baking sheet in the oven, close the door and leave for 15 minutes. Turn down the heat to 190°C/375°F/Gas Mark 5 and leave to bake for 30 minutes longer. The loaf, when properly cooked, should have a nice brown crust and should sound hollow when tapped on the bottom.

notes

Chicory *is a long, torpedo-shaped shoot, almost white, with pale yellow or green tips to the tightly packed leaves. It has a fresh, slightly bitter taste and can be used raw in salads or cooked as a vegetable. It is now widely available for most of the year.*

BRAISED CHICORY

6 small or 3 large heads of chicory, weighing about 750 g/1½ lb
2 tbsp olive oil
50 g/2 oz butter
2 tsp sugar
salt and freshly ground black pepper
juice of 1 lemon

1 Heat the oven to 180°C/350°F/Gas Mark 4. Cut a small piece of the hard stalk end of each head of chicory. If using large ones, cut each in half lengthways.
2 Pour the oil into a shallow ovenproof dish, casserole or pan and arrange the chicory in one layer. If using halved large heads, place cut-side down.
3 Dot with the butter and sprinkle over the sugar, salt and pepper to taste. Sprinkle over the lemon juice and cover with either a lid or kitchen foil.
4 Bake at the bottom of the preheated oven for 1½–2 hours or until it is cooked and tender. (You can cook it at the same time as the lamb in the following recipe, on a lower shelf in the oven.)
5 Put the hot chicory on warmed plates and pour over the cooking juices. Serve with home-made bread (or other good bread) to mop up the delicious juice.

ROASTED SHOULDER OF LAMB WITH GARLIC, ROSEMARY AND LEMON

a large shoulder of lamb weighing about 1.8–2 kg/4–4½lb (the knuckle cut off by the butcher and reserved)
2 large cloves garlic, peeled and cut into long matchstick pieces
2 × 5-cm/2-in strips of finely peeled lemon rind, cut diagonally into matchstick pieces
1 heaped tsp rosemary, fresh or dried
900 ml/1½ pt water
salt and freshly ground black pepper
1 tbsp flour
juice of ½ lemon

1 Heat the oven to 180°C/350°F/ Gas Mark 4.
2 With a little pointed knife make incisions all over the piece of meat about 5 cm/2 in apart and about 2.5 cm/1 in deep.
3 Poke a 'matchstick' of garlic and lemon rind into each incision in the meat, with a blade or two of rosemary. Place the meat in a roasting tin, preferably on a metal trivet if you have one.
4 Season to taste with salt and pepper. Roast near the top of the preheated oven for 2 hours, basting occasionally.
5 Meanwhile, simmer the knuckle in the water, seasoned to taste with salt and pepper, for 1 hour. Discard the bone and make the liquid up to 500 ml/1 pt with water if too much has evaporated.

6 When the meat is cooked, place it on a heated serving dish in a warm place to 'rest', while you make the gravy and eat the first course.
7 For the gravy, pour off most of the fat from the roasting tin and discard. Place the roasting tin over a medium heat on top of the stove and stir the flour into the remaining fat. Cook for 1 minute than add the stock from the knuckle and bring to the boil, stirring all the time and scratching up any tasty bits from the corners of the pan. Simmer for 2 minutes and then pour through a sieve into a small saucepan. This will get rid of any lumps. Add the lemon juice and season with more salt and pepper if necessary. Reheat at the last minute and pour into a heated jug or gravy boat.
8 Bring the meat to the table on a serving dish to carve and serve with the potatoes in the following recipe. It isn't really necessary to serve another vegetable after having had a vegetable first course, but if you like, peas or broad beans would go very well.

notes

Rosemary, *which grows wild all over the Mediterranean, has a strong, aromatic flavour reminiscent of the smell of pine trees in summer. It is mostly associated with lamb, but is pleasant with other strongly flavoured meats and vegetable dishes too. It should be used sparingly, however, and only in cooked dishes, as the small spiky leaves are too hard and the flavour too dominant to be eaten raw, although the little lavender-coloured flowers can be used in salads or as a garnish.*

Ristorante «IL NOCE»
di Ramella Dominica & c s.d.f.
VIA Buenos Aires s.n.c.
REZZO (IM) traz. CENOVA
P. IVA e C. F. 00900560087

Although it is certainly a treat to eat occasionally in a rather posh restaurant I have found that invariably in France and Italy the best food is to be had in the small unpretentious family-run establishments. These are sometimes off the beaten track, but fun to look for and well worth the search, like 'Il Noce' in the Ligurian hilltown of Cenova, where we enjoyed a memorable meal during a tremendous electric summer storm.

POTATOES DAUPHINOISE

1.35 kg/3 lb waxy potatoes
300 ml/10 fl oz milk
115 g/4 oz butter
1 scant tsp grated nutmeg
salt and freshly ground black
pepper
1 clove garlic, peeled and crushed
115 g/4 oz grated Gruyère cheese

1 Heat the oven to 180°C/350°F/
Gas Mark 4. Peel the potatoes and
slice them across into thin slices. Do
not wash them as this would
remove the starch which makes the
finished dish so creamy.
2 In a medium saucepan heat the
milk with half the butter, the nutmeg
and salt and pepper to taste over a
low heat. When it reaches boiling
point, turn down the heat as low as
you can get it, add the potatoes
and simmer for 10 minutes stirring
occasionally.
3 Use the remaining butter to
grease a shallow ovenproof dish
(preferably one that will fit on a shelf
next to the dish you are cooking the
chicory in).
4 Mix the crushed garlic into the
potato mixture, then pour it all into
the buttered dish. Sprinkle over the
grated cheese and bake for 2 hours
in the preheated oven. If cooking
these potatoes under the meat, just
turn off the heat when they are done
and leave them in the oven while
you eat the first course.

CELERY WITH ALMOND CHEESE AND MANGO CHUTNEY

50 g/2 oz slivered blanched
almonds, toasted under a hot grill
until golden
140 g/5 oz cream cheese
salt and freshly ground black
pepper
6 large sticks celery, washed and
dried well
ready-prepared mango chutney

1 Mash the cream cheese, add the
almonds, and mix well together,
then season to taste with salt and
pepper. Mix with a fork until
spreadable.
2 Divide this mixture among the
celery sticks, spreading into the
hollow side and smoothing it with a
knife.
3 Slice each cheese-filled stick of
celery across into 2.5-cm/1-in
sections and arrange on small
plates. Spoon a little mango
chutney on to each plate.

Nutmeg is the fruit of an
evergreen myrtle native to
Indonesia. Its warm gently
spicy flavour has been
universally popular for both
sweet and savoury dishes for
centuries. Best bought whole
and grated as needed. I buy
mine in wholefood shops,
where they are generally
much cheaper.

notes

menu 2

MELON IN GARLIC VINAIGRETTE

DEEP-FRIED CALAMARI RINGS

SOUFFLÉ 'POPEYE'

*WARM COMPOTE OF
DRIED FRUITS*

MELON IN GARLIC VINAIGRETTE

1 small ripe melon, such as
honeydew, ogen, cantaloupe etc
(type in season)
1 quantity vinaigrette dressing
(page 29) made with 1 clove
crushed garlic
about 1 small or ½ large cos
lettuce, or any fresh, seasonal
salad greens, washed, drained
and shredded

1 Peel the melon and discard the
seeds. Cut into cubes or balls (if you
have a melon baller, and the time
and energy). Place in a bowl, pour
over the dressing and stir. Cover
closely with kitchen film and chill for
at least 1 hour.
2 Divide the shredded salad greens
between six plates or pretty bowls.
Divide the melon between these
and drizzle the dressing from the
bowl over them.

DEEP-FRIED CALAMARI RINGS

1.35 kg/3 lb small squid, or 900 g/
2 lb if bought ready cleaned
seasoned flour
vegetable oil for deep frying
salt
6 lemon wedges

1 Clean the squid if not already
done (see note) and cut across the
'sacs' into 1-cm/½-in sections. Toss
these rings, and the tentacles if you
have them (you won't if you have

bought the squid ready cleaned) to
coat them in the seasoned flour: this
is most easily done in a plastic bag.
2 Heat the oil until smoking in a
large deep pan or deep-fat fryer,
and fry in small batches until golden
brown and crisp. (I do this, like so
many other jobs, in my large iron
two-handled wok: it is a nice heavy
one and is in fact from an Indian
shop.) As the rings are cooked, lift
them out with a slotted spoon, drain
on crumpled kitchen paper and
keep warm in a low oven until you
have cooked them all.
3 Sprinkle with salt to taste and
divide between six heated plates.
Serve with lemon wedges.

SOUFFLÉ 'POPEYE'

450 g/1 lb fresh leaf spinach, thick
stems removed and discarded (or
saved to go in a soup at a later
date)
85 g/3 oz butter
50 g/2 oz flour
300 ml/10 fl oz milk
salt and freshly ground black
pepper
½ tsp freshly grated nutmeg
breadcrumbs from 1 medium slice
of stale white bread
6 eggs, separated

1 Wash the spinach thoroughly. Put
it in a medium, lidded saucepan in
only the water that clings to the
leaves after washing it, cover and
cook over a medium heat, shaking
the pan fairly often, until the leaves
have completely wilted. This will
take about 3 minutes: watch ▷

notes

*Squid come in many sizes and
are available fresh or frozen
from good fishmongers. Many
people are nervous about eating
squid for the first time, and
even more so about cooking it.
This is hardly surprising. This
cephalopod mollusc, cousin to
the terrifying octopus, is
certainly not very appealing to
look at in its raw unprepared
state, but it is nevertheless
extremely delicious to eat.
Luckily some fishmongers sell
them ready prepared and
cleaned. If not, this is how to
deal with the whole creature:
1 Take hold of the sac-shaped
body in one hand and the head
and tentacles in the other and
pull the two pieces apart: the
head will come away easily,
bringing with it the long almost
transparent taper-like backbone
and the rest of the innards.
2 Now cut off the tentacles
where they meet the head.
Discard the head (easily
recognizable by the gruesome
bulbous eyes on either side),
the attached bone and innards.
3 The sac will probably have a
thin purplish skin covering it:
this comes off easily and is
discarded. Wash the sac and
tentacles thoroughly under
running water.*

◁ constantly and be careful not to let it burn. For the last few seconds of cooking time, take the lid off the pan and allow any remaining moisture to evaporate. Either chop the cooked spinach finely or reduce to a purée in a liquidizer or food processor.

2 Place a baking sheet in the middle of the oven and heat to 200°C/400°F/Gas Mark 6.

3 Melt 50 g/2 oz of the butter in a medium saucepan and add the flour. Cook, stirring constantly, for 2–3 minutes. Add the milk and bring to the boil, stirring constantly and making sure that no lumps form. When the sauce is boiling, turn down the heat to low. Add salt and pepper to taste and the nutmeg and simmer, stirring occasionally, for 5 minutes. Allow to cool slightly.

4 Use the remaining 30 g/1 oz butter to thoroughly grease a 1.75-litre/3-pt straight-sided soufflé dish. Tip the breadcrumbs and swirl around to coat the bottom and sides. Tip out the excess. (This will help the soufflé to slide up the sides of the dish as it rises, without sticking.)

5 Mix the spinach and the egg yolks into the cooled white sauce and tip into a large bowl.

6 In another large bowl, whisk the egg whites with a pinch of salt until stiff but not dry-looking. Fold a spoonful of this into the spinach mixture to slacken it, using an 'in and over' motion with a metal spoon. The intention is to keep as much air in the mixture as possible. As the air bubbles expand with the heat, the soufflé will rise. Working as quickly and gently as possible,

fold in the rest of the beaten egg white.

7 Pour the mixture into the prepared dish and place immediately in the hot oven on the baking sheet and close the door quickly.

8 The soufflé will take about 25 minutes to cook, depending on your oven. The cooked soufflé should be well risen and firm to the touch, with just a hint of 'wobble' left in it, when pressed on the top with a finger. Do not over-cook it: it is better if the soufflé is a little soft inside rather than too dry.

9 Spoon the soufflé immediately on to warm plates. Some people like to serve a sauce with a soufflé, but if it is perfectly cooked and not dried out, this should not be necessary.

WARM COMPOTE OF DRIED FRUITS

1 jasmine or Earl Grey teabag
1.1 litres/2 pt boiling water
350 g/12 oz dried apricots
350 g/12 oz dried prunes
350 g/12 oz raisins
575 ml/1 pt unsweetened pure orange juice
6 split cardamom pods
1 × 4-cm/1½-in piece of stick cinnamon
natural yoghurt (optional)

1 Place the teabag in a large bowl and pour over the boiling water. Leave for about 5 minutes. Give the teabag a little squeeze with the back of a spoon, then remove it and discard.

2 Put all the dried fruit in the tea and

Scented teas *like jasmine, Earl Grey and Lapsang Souchong with its distinctive smoky flavour are excellent for use as cooking liquids; even everyday Indian tea makes a good substitute for beer or wine in stews and casseroles. I now find that many of my friends often prefer a cup of light scented tea to coffee after dinner. I myself like camomile tea. I have a pretty set of small blue and white Victorian cups and saucers which are ideal for either tea or coffee.*

There are many *kinds of orange juice now on sale, so it is important to read the ingredients on the package or bottle carefully. I buy the kind sold in rectangular cardboard cartons, always checking that it does not contain any sugar or other additives.*

Cinnamon *is readily available powdered, but it has more flavour in stick form. These sticks are in fact the bark of an evergreen laurel native to Sri Lanka.*

leave covered for at least 12 hours or overnight.
3 Drain the fruit and place in a medium saucepan with the orange juice, cardamom pods and a piece of cinnamon stick. Bring to the boil, then turn down the heat and simmer, uncovered, over a low heat for about 30 minutes. The fruit should then be tender and the juice reduced to make a really delicious syrup. Watch carefully near to the end of the cooking time that the pan

doesn't boil dry and the fruit catch on the bottom, however. If the liquid levels look too low, add a little water. Cool a little then tip into a serving dish, or individual bowls.
4 Serve warm, as it is, or with some chilled yoghurt: the thick Greek style is particularly good. I have purposely given quantities in this recipe for more than six normal servings, as the leftovers make a perfect breakfast next day for a deserving cook.

menu 3

*MISS BAILEY'S
PUDDING WITH GRAVY*

BOILED SALT BRISKET OF BEEF

PEASE PUDDING

SYLLABUB

MISS BAILEY'S PUDDING WITH GRAVY

2 large onions, peeled and chopped
30 g/1 oz beef dripping (Miss Hilda Bailey would have insisted on dripping, but use lard if you have none)
1 heaped tbsp cooked white rice
85 g/3 oz fresh white breadcrumbs
1 heaped tbsp grated suet
1 level tbsp porridge oats
½ tsp dried sage (1 tsp if using fresh)
½ tsp dried thyme (1 tsp if using fresh)
salt and freshly ground black pepper
2 eggs
115 g/4 oz plain white flour
300 ml/10 fl oz milk

1 Put the onions in a small saucepan and add enough cold water to not quite cover them. Cook, uncovered, over a moderate heat for about 15 minutes or until the onions are soft and the water has all evaporated. Watch carefully when they are almost cooked and be careful that they do not burn.

2 Heat the oven to 220°C/425°F/ Gas Mark 7 and put the dripping (or lard) into a medium-sized metal roasting tin, ovenproof dish or large round metal flan tin (obviously not the loose-bottomed kind).

3 In a large bowl, mix together the cooked onions, the rice, the breadcrumbs, suet, oats, sage and thyme, and season well with salt and pepper.

4 Beat the eggs with the flour and milk to make a smooth batter and mix this with the onion mixture. (It doesn't seem to make much difference if you make the batter in advance and leave it to rest.)

5 Pour the mixture into the hot fat in the pan and bake for 15 minutes in the centre of the oven, then turn down the heat to 180°C/350°F/Gas Mark 4 and cook for another 45 minutes.

6 Serve cut into squares or wedges on warmed plates, with some of the gravy from the following recipe.

notes

This is a genuine old Yorkshire recipe. Miss Bailey died in the 1960s, and was already quite old when I first knew her. This recipe was given to her by her mother who probably got it from hers, so it is certainly over a hundred years old to my knowledge, and is probably very much older. Many such savoury puddings were popular in Victorian times, in both town and country, as they took the edge off the appetite before the expensive meat course was served. These puddings were always served like this as a first course, never with the meat, and many hungry children were tricked into almost losing their appetite completely before the meat was on the table by the old saying, ''Im as eats most puddin' gets most meat' (to be read with a Yorkshire accent).

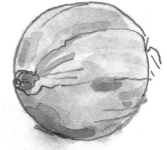

Doctors constantly tell us not to eat too much red meat, and many people have at last got away from the idea that a 'proper meal' must be based on meat. There is not a lot of meat in this book and where it is used the quantities are relatively small compared with the rest of the ingredients. For an occasional treat, however, a 'meat and two veg' dinner is delicious. It is not necessary to serve mountains of meat if the accompanying vegetables are well cooked and tempting, or if you serve a substantial first course like Miss Bailey's Pudding. Boiled meat has been rather out of fashion in recent years, but can be tastier than roasted meat. Serve the brisket with Pease Pudding, and plain boiled potatoes and carrots. Hand hot English mustard and horseradish sauce separately for those who like them.

BOILED SALT BRISKET OF BEEF

A piece of salted brisket of beef weighing about 1 kg/2¼ lb
2 onions
8 whole cloves
freshly grated nutmeg
salt and freshly ground black pepper
1 tbsp (or more) flour, mixed to a smooth paste with a little cold water

1 Cut the onions into quarters, leaving on the skins (they add a rich colour to the gravy) and stick a clove into each piece.
2 Place the beef, surrounded by the onions, in a lidded saucepan which fits the piece of meat quite snuggly. Pour over enough cold water to just cover and season well with nutmeg, salt and pepper.
3 Bring to the boil and then simmer over the lowest possible heat for 2½ hours, tightly covered. Skim away any scum which rises to the surface at the beginning of the cooking time (but you probably won't get much with salted beef).
4 Remove the meat and keep warm. Strain the cooking liquid and discard the onion. Return the stock to the pan and reduce by rapid boiling to just over 575 ml/1 pt. Mix a little of the hot stock with the flour and water mixture and return this to the pan. Simmer, stirring, until thickened. If you like your gravy thicker, add more flour and water. Simmer for about 5 minutes to cook the flour, and check the seasonings.
5 Slice the beef and serve on fresh heated plates.

PEASE PUDDING

250 g/8.82 oz 'quick-soak' dried peas
55 g/2 oz butter
1 egg, beaten
salt and freshly ground black pepper
1 tbsp chopped fresh mint (optional)
sprig of mint to garnish (if available)

1 Soak the peas for 2 hours (or, if you are using ordinary dried peas, according to the instructions on the packet) in 850 ml/1½ pt boiling water.
2 Drain and place in a medium saucepan with 425 ml/15 fl oz boiling water and 1 level tsp salt. Bring to the boil and simmer over a low heat, uncovered, for 15–20 minutes (or according to the instructions on the packet) until all the water has been absorbed and the peas are tender.
3 Mash the peas with a fork, and while still hot, mix in half the butter and season to taste with salt and pepper. When the mixture has cooled a little, mix in the beaten egg and the mint (if liked).
4 Grease a 850 ml/1½ pt pudding bowl with the remaining butter and fill with the pea mixture.
5 Cover the bowl tightly with kitchen foil and steam over gently boiling water for 1 hour.
6 Either turn out on to a warm plate and decorate with a sprig of fresh mint (if available), or serve from the bowl.

SYLLABUB

150 ml/5 fl oz sherry (whatever kind you have, or – if you are buying it specially – whichever sort you are going to enjoy finishing the rest of the bottle of)
juice and finely peeled rind of 1 large lemon
50 g/2 oz sugar
grated nutmeg
300 ml/10 fl oz double cream

1 Place the sherry, lemon juice and rind in a bowl, cover with kitchen film and chill overnight or for at least 6 hours.
2 Strain into another bowl and discard the peel. Add the sugar and stir until dissolved. Add a little grated nutmeg to taste and then gradually stir in the cream.
3 Using an electric beater or a wire whisk, beat the mixture until it forms soft peaks. Do not over-beat, or the mixture might curdle.
4 Spoon into six glasses or pretty dishes and chill for about 2 hours.

Syllabubs were popular with the Elizabethans, but their syllabubs were simply a foamy drink made by milking the cow straight into a cup or bowl of wine or cider. By the eighteenth century it had become a more sophisticated creamy dessert with whipped cream and perhaps fruit juices. A traditional syllabub now usually contains brandy as well as sherry, but I think that this recipe is just as nice without.

SIMPLE
PLEASURES

menu 4

CHILLED TOMATO SOUP

*LITTLE POTATO AND ONION PIES
WITH A SAGE SUET CRUST*

HONEYED FRUIT SALAD

Honey is an ancient and useful food and was once the only form of sweetening. Its preservative qualities are demonstrated in its use in ancient times for embalming bodies. We ate lots of delicious honey in Yugoslavia while camping by a lake high in the beautiful mountainous region of Slovenia, a part of the country which is famous for the excellence of its honey and which exports bees all over the world.

notes

Worcestershire sauce is a hot spicy sauce which comes ready prepared in bottles and is made to an old Indian recipe. A few drops will give a little zest to a savoury dish, but it should be used sparingly as its taste is very distinctive and can be overpowering if used too generously. It is perhaps best known as the main flavouring in a Bloody Mary cocktail.

CHILLED TOMATO SOUP

450 ml/15 fl oz chicken stock (see page 17) or vegetable stock
450 ml/15 fl oz pure tomato juice (available in cans, jars or cardboard cartons)
6 spring onions, trimmed and finely chopped
2 cloves garlic, peeled and crushed
450 g/1 lb tomatoes, peeled, deseeded and chopped
salt and freshly ground black pepper
dash of Worcestershire sauce (optional)
finely chopped fresh basil, chives or parsley (as available)

1 Mix the stock (warming it a little first if at all jellied) with the tomato juice, chopped onion, garlic and tomatoes. Season to taste with salt and pepper and add a small dash of Worcestershire sauce if you like it – but do use it sparingly so as not to drown the flavour of the tomatoes. Chill for at least 4 hours.
2 Serve in chilled bowls or soup dishes, sprinkled with the chopped herbs.

LITTLE POTATO AND ONION PIES WITH A SAGE SUET CRUST

1.35 kg/3 lb potatoes
3 medium or 2 large onions, peeled and chopped
3 tbsp vegetable oil
about 850 ml/1½ pt milk
salt and freshly ground black pepper
oil for greasing pie dishes
1 quantity of suet pastry (see page 20), substituting for the grated lemon peel 1 tsp dried sage (or 1½ tsp fresh sage)

1 Peel the potatoes and cut them into 2.5-cm/1-in cubes. Do not rinse them or you will remove the starch which thickens the sauce.
2 In a medium saucepan cook the onions in the oil over a medium heat or until soft. Add the potatoes and continue to cook for 2–3 minutes, stirring constantly. Add the milk, which should just not quite cover the potatoes in the pan. Bring to the boil, turn down the heat to low, season to taste with salt and pepper and simmer, uncovered, for about 15 minutes, stirring occasionally, or until the potatoes are tender and the milk has turned into a creamy sauce. Meanwhile, preheat the oven to 230°C/425°F/ Gas Mark 7.
3 Divide the mixture between six lightly oiled small ovenproof pie dishes or one large one and leave to cool slightly.
4 Divide the pastry into six equal portions and roll out 'lids' to fit over

the potato mixture in the pie dishes (or roll out one big 'lid' if making one large pie).

5 Bake the pies in the preheated oven for about 20 minutes, or until the pastry is cooked and crisp on top.

6 Serve individual pies in their dishes, or serve a big one out on to heated plates. I serve broccoli and carrots with these pies, but any fresh vegetables would go equally well.

HONEYED FRUIT SALAD

juice of 1 large or 2 small oranges
1 generous tbsp of runny honey (or more if liked)
2 crisp dessert apples
225 g/8 oz grapes
2 small peaches, or 225 g/8 oz fresh strawberries, or 225 g/8 oz raspberries (thawed if frozen – see method)
1 ripe mango (optional)

1 Put the orange juice in an attractive bowl and stir in the honey until well mixed.

2 Wash and core the apples, but leave on the skins. (Red-skinned apples look nice if you are using green grapes, and green-skinned ones if using black grapes.) Cut the apples into small cubes measuring about 1 cm/½ in and stir these into the orange juice and honey. Do this quickly and they will not discolour.

3 Wash the grapes and pick them off the stem. Deseed them if you think it is really necessary and add

them to the bowl.

4 Cut the peaches in half, remove the stones, skin them if you feel you must (I don't), and cut the flesh into 1-cm/½-in cubes. If you are using strawberries, hull and quarter them (do not use frozen strawberries, the 'defrost' in the ingredients refers only to raspberries, which are quite good frozen). Add to the bowl.

5 If using a mango, remove the flesh from the skin and the stone as best you can. It doesn't matter if you make a messy job – mangos are not easy to deal with, but work over a bowl to collect the juice. Chop the flesh small and add, with any juice, to the bowl.

6 Chill for at least 2 hours before serving.

A few wild flowers in a simple glass vase or even a jam jar so that their stems show as well make an enchanting table decoration, much more so than a careful arrangement, and cost nothing. If there are no wild flowers around a bunch of grasses or other greenery can look just as nice. In autumn and winter a bowl of fallen leaves with perhaps some conkers and acorns will make an attractive and seasonal centrepiece for the table.

menu 5

PASTA WITH TOMATO CREAM SAUCE

GRILLED TROUT
WITH LEEKS AND BACON

QUEEN OF PUDDINGS

LE SHOPPING

ÎLE DE FRANCE

Through modern fish farming techniques trout is no longer the luxury food it once was and is now in fact cheaper than other fish that were at one time considered quite ordinary. Not only do I love its delicious subtle flavour, but I enjoy cooking it more than other fish as it leaves no fishy smell in the house. Farmed trout is excellent eating, though not nearly so good as wild trout.

notes

To skin tomatoes *easily, put them in a bowl and cover them with boiling water. After 2 minutes drain them; the skins will slip off easily, or you can help them with a sharp knife. The sauce will be much nicer if you do skin the tomatoes as you will not have any little pieces of peel in it to spoil the texture.*

PASTA WITH TOMATO CREAM SAUCE

The sauce
50 g/2 oz butter
900 g/2 lb tomatoes, washed, skinned and roughly chopped
2 cloves garlic, peeled and crushed
300 ml/10 fl oz single cream
salt and freshly ground black pepper
You will also need
450 g/1 lb dried pasta, any shape you fancy (550 g/1¼ lb or more for large appetites, if using fresh)
finely chopped fresh parsley, or (much better) fresh basil, if available

1 First make the sauce. Melt the butter in a medium saucepan and cook the tomatoes over a low heat, stirring occasionally, for about 5 minutes or until the tomatoes have softened.
2 Add the garlic and cream and season to taste with salt and pepper. Bring to the boil and simmer over a low heat for about 3–4 minutes, stirring occasionally.
3 Bring a large pan of salted water to the boil and cook the pasta until 'al dente'.
4 Reheat the sauce. Drain the pasta and pour over the sauce. Toss together until well amalgamated.
5 Serve in hot bowls or dishes, sprinkled with the chopped herbs. This pasta does not need Parmesan cheese sprinkled over it, as it has a delicate subtle flavour which is drowned by the strong flavour of Parmesan.

GRILLED TROUT WITH LEEKS AND BACON

170 g/6 oz chopped streaky bacon (bacon 'pieces' are ideal, smoked ones even better)
1 tbsp vegetable oil
675 g/1½ lb leeks, trimmed, thoroughly washed and cut across into about 1-cm/½-in slices
freshly ground black pepper
6 medium-sized trout, gutted
55 g/2 oz melted butter
salt and freshly ground black pepper
6 sprigs of parsley, or dill (if available)
6 slices of lemon

1 In a medium lidded saucepan, cook the bacon in the oil over a low heat, stirring, until the bacon is cooked and the fat runs.
2 Add the leeks and season well with pepper – there will probably be enough salt in the bacon. Cover the pan tightly and cook over a low heat, shaking the pan occasionally, for about 10–12 minutes or until the leeks are cooked.
3 Meanwhile, turn the grill on to high, and brush the fish inside and out with the melted butter, seasoning well inside and out with salt and pepper. Slip a sprig of parsley or dill and a slice of lemon inside the cavity of each fish.
4 Place the fish on a foil-lined grill pan and cook under the hot grill for about 7 minutes each side, or until done.
5 Place a whole fish with some of the leek and bacon mixture on each warmed plate.

QUEEN OF PUDDINGS

85 g/3 oz fresh white breadcrumbs
100 g/3½ oz caster sugar
grated rind of 1 small lemon
450 ml/15 fl oz milk
55 g/2 oz butter
3 eggs, separated
2 tbsp warmed apricot or
raspberry jam

1 Put the breadcrumbs with 40 g/ 1½ oz of the sugar and the lemon rind in a bowl.

2 Put the milk and 40 g/1½ oz of the butter in a medium saucepan and heat gently over a low heat, just until the butter is melted and the milk is slightly warm. Pour on to the breadcrumb mixture and leave to stand for 15 minutes for the crumbs to swell and absorb the milk. Meanwhile, heat the oven to 190°C/375°F/Gas Mark 5. Lightly beat the egg yolks and stir into the breadcrumb mixture.

3 Grease a 850-ml–1.1-litre/ 1½–2-pt shallow ovenproof baking dish with the remaining 15 g/½ oz butter and pour in the mixture.

4 Bake in the centre of the preheated oven for 30–35 minutes or until set. Remove from the oven and carefully spread with the jam.

5 Whisk the egg whites until they stand in peaks and gradually add the remaining sugar, a little at a time. Whisk again until stiff.

6 Cover the top of the jam with the meringue and fork it up into little rough peaks all over.

7 Return to the oven and bake for 10–12 minutes more.

8 Serve hot, warm or even chilled.

One of the nicest of the many simple pleasures I enjoy is relaxing with a glass of wine at the end of a hard day's work. It seems to taste even nicer served from an attractive jug, as *vino locale* is often served in small Italian restaurants. This is an elegant and original way of offering your home-made and supermarket wines to guests – and it gives cheaper wines the chance to breathe.

CHAPTER 4

Mean and Lean

FOR MOST OF MY life – that is, up until six years ago – I was always regarded as skinny; I also smoked like two or three factory chimneys. Now I no longer smoke and I am no longer regarded as skinny. Where once people would say, 'I wish I were slim like you' (meaning 'God, isn't he thin?'), they are now more prone to say, 'Don't you look well!' (meaning '*Hasn't* he put on weight!'). I certainly don't now consider myself fat, but I liked being skinny, and every year as the time approaches for migration to warmer climates, the thought of shedding clothes sends me into a cold panic about being overweight. When I see the reflection in my cruel full-length mirror of the curves induced by sustaining winter food I am goaded into losing some weight.

Crash diets might work for a while, but the inches tend to go back on more quickly than they disappeared once you return to normal eating. The most successful way to get into better shape is to slowly and methodically cut down on certain 'fattening' foods and to combine a sensible diet with some regular exercise. Exercise, I firmly believe, is more important than the diet as it tones up the muscles and makes your body noticeably more streamlined by holding some bits in, and moving other bits around to more appealing places, even if you weigh the same.

Most scientifically worked out diets will tell you to cut down on fat and sugar as much as possible and to eat regular meals at sensible times. Skipping a meal like breakfast is dangerous as you then tend to feel ravenous and resort to snacks like sweets and crisps which are bursting with empty calories. Only eat when you know you can be fully in control of your choice of food.

The two things which seem to frighten people most when they are thinking about trying to lose weight, is that they will be hungry all the time and that they will have to spend a lot more money on food – but this need not be so.

It is not difficult to diet without feeling hungry if you eat lots of food which is high in fibre, but low in fats and sugar. Fresh fruit and vegetables are generally very low in the things which make you fat, but there are a few exceptions to every rule and there are plenty of books available written by experts to tell you exactly what these are. It is also a good idea to prepare food that is particularly tasty, as you can

POSEIDON SURVEYS HIS DOMAINE

easily devour large quantities of food if it is bland and uninteresting before you have noticed that you are eating at all.

This chapter is in no way intended as a complete weight-loss diet, but is simply menus for occasions when you want to produce a special meal without anyone noticing it is a slimmers' meal; without spending much money; and without anyone leaving the table feeling hungry. The meals are based mainly on seafoods, vegetables and fruit, and contain the minimum of fat and sugar. A filling first course is the perfect way to start a 'diet' meal. A thick soup of puréed vegetables is tasty, nourishing and filling, and very low in calories. Fish plays an important part in this chapter, not only because I love it, but because it is very high in nutrients and very low in harmful fats.

I am lucky because I do not have a sweet tooth and don't get tempted by chocolate bars, but I do occasionally long for a lamb chop with lots of crispy delicious fat, or to smother some new potatoes or asparagus in lashings of butter, but when I do, if I am trying to lose some weight, I think of the beaches of Australia, Italy or Yugoslavia and all the lean brown healthy-looking bodies – and I cook some of these recipes instead.

MEAN
AND LEAN

menu 1

RICOTTA AND OLIVE PÂTÉ

CURRIED MUSSELS

VEGETABLE COUSCOUS

*ORANGE AND MANGO YOGHURT MOUSSE
WITH APRICOT SAUCE*

RICOTTA AND OLIVE PÂTÉ

225 g/8 oz ricotta cheese
115 g/4 oz black olives, stoned
and finely chopped
2 cloves garlic, peeled and
crushed
salt and freshly ground black
pepper

1 Mash the cheese well with a fork
and mix in the chopped olives,
reserving a few for garnish. Mix in
the garlic and season to taste with
salt and pepper. (This can all be
done in a food processor.)
2 Pack the mixture into an attractive
dish or bowl and smooth over the
top. Alternatively, pile into a mound
on a pretty plate. Scatter over the
reserved olive pieces. Chill for at
least 1 and up to 24 hours for the
flavours to develop.
3 Serve with wholemeal savoury
biscuits, low-calorie crackers or just
sticks of celery.

CURRIED MUSSELS

2 kg/4½ lb live mussels in shells
1 medium onion, peeled and
chopped
850 ml/1½ pt chicken stock (see
page 17), or fish stock
2 tsp curry powder (or more)
salt and freshly ground black
pepper
finely chopped parsley or
coriander to garnish

1 Scrub the mussels thoroughly in
cold water, removing any barnacles

with a sharp knife. Rinse and drain.
Using your thumb and the blade of
a knife, strip away any 'beard'
which protrudes from the straight
side of the shell. Rinse again in
running water.
2 Leave the mussels to soak in cold
water for at least 1 hour to remove
any traces of mud or sand. Change
the water at least three times during
this soaking period. Discard any
mussels that are not firmly closed.
3 Put the onion in a large lidded
saucepan with the stock, bring to
the boil and simmer, covered, over
a low heat for 5 minutes.
4 Add the curry powder (more if you
think you would like the mussels
really hot)
5 Drain the mussels. Any that
remain open after being given a
sharp tap with a knife should be
discarded.
6 Tip the mussels into the pan, turn
up the heat to full and, once the
liquid has returned to the boil, cover
the pan tightly with a lid. Cook,
shaking occasionally, for about 5
minutes, by which time all the
mussels should have opened. Do
not overcook, or the mussels will
toughen and become rubbery.
Discard any which have remained
shut.
7 Divide the mussels and the liquid
between six hot soup plates and
sprinkle with the chopped herb.
Serve immediately. An empty shell
is useful for scooping up the juices —
or provide soup spoons for the job.

notes

*Ricotta is an Italian fresh soft
cheese made from the whey of
cows' milk. It is low in fat and
useful for both sweet and
savoury dishes, having a mild
creamy taste. It is sold in
Italian grocers, good
delicatessens and large
supermarkets. Be sure to buy it
absolutely fresh, or it will have
a rancid aftertaste.*

*Mussels are one of the very
few inexpensive luxury foods
and are to me among the
tastiest of shellfish. These
delicious molluscs in their
beautiful oval shells the colour
of blue-black ink are best
known as the main ingredient
in the popular French moules
marinière, but are very
versatile and can be used in all
sorts of ways. Frozen mussels
are acceptable in some dishes
but once you have prepared
fresh mussels in their shells,
you will buy them again and
again. (Many fishmongers
now sell mussels already
cleaned, which makes the job
very much quicker
and easier.)*

Fresh fruit and vegetables are not only delicious but are particular friends for anyone trying to lose weight. Eaten raw they will fill you up without making you fat.

VEGETABLE COUSCOUS

1 × 387-g/14-oz can of tomatoes
2 large onions, peeled and
chopped
170 g/6 oz mushrooms, sliced
2 cloves garlic, peeled and
crushed
1 tbsp finely chopped parsley (or
oregano or basil)
salt and freshly ground black
pepper
350 g/12 oz couscous
1 small cauliflower, trimmed and
cut into florets
450 g/1 lb broccoli (or other fresh
green vegetable in season),
washed and prepared for cooking

1 Place the canned tomatoes, with
their juice and the onions,
mushrooms, garlic and the parsley
in a medium saucepan and season
to taste with salt and pepper.
2 Simmer, covered, over a low heat
for 30 minutes.
3 Put the couscous with 350 ml/12 fl
oz of water into a medium
saucepan and place the pan over a
low heat, stirring constantly, for 2–3
minutes, or until the water has all
been absorbed.
4 Line the top of a steamer with two
layers of butter muslin and tip in the
couscous. Steam over boiling water
for 20 minutes.
5 Just before serving the couscous,
cook the cauliflower and the other
vegetable in salted boiling water, or
steam until just tender.
6 Divide the couscous between six
warmed plates, with some of the
tomato mixture and the vegetables
on the other side of the plate.

ORANGE AND MANGO YOGHURT MOUSSE WITH APRICOT SAUCE

1 ripe mango
450 ml/15 fl oz low-fat natural
yoghurt
1 sachet of powdered gelatine
50 ml/2 fl oz unsweetened pure
orange juice
1 peach or nectarine (optional)
1 egg white
1 quantity of apricot purée (see
Fromage Blanc with Fruit Purées,
page 113), thinned with a little
water

1 Remove all the flesh from the skin
and stone of mango as best you
can. (This is always a messy job so
do it over a bowl to catch the juice.)
2 Liquidize the flesh with the
yoghurt, and tip into a medium
sized bowl.
3 Dissolve the gelatine in the
orange juice (see page 21) and mix
this into the yoghurt and fruit
mixture.
4 Peel the peach or nectarine (if
used) and remove the stone; cut the
flesh into small pieces and stir this
into the mixture in the bowl.
5 Beat the egg white until stiff but
not dry, fold into the fruit mixture
and pour into six small moulds,
glasses or bowls. Leave to set for
3–4 hours, or about 6 hours if you
wish to turn the mousses out.
6 Pour a little of the apricot sauce
over the mousses, or turn out on to
chilled plates by dipping the moulds
into hot water, and spoon a little of
the sauce next to them.

notes

*Couscous is a popular North
African dish (also much eaten
in France) which is a stew of
meat or fish and vegetables
served alongside a staple of
couscous grains. These look
like tiny grains of rice, but are
in fact made from hard wheat
and water, and are therefore
really a close relative of pasta.
Couscous is available from
good delicatessens and
Continental grocers.*

*You do not need to add the
peach or the nectarine – this
mousse is very nice without it;
but this is a versatile recipe that
can be made with or without
pieces of fruit (other kinds can
of course be substituted) and
with different kinds of fruit
purées. It is only necessary to
remember that 1 sachet of
gelatine will set about 575
ml/1 pt of liquid. (This does
not include the whisked egg
white, which is mostly air.)*

MEAN
AND LEAN

menu 2

JELLIED TOMATO SALAD

CHICKEN AND HERB RISOTTO

GRAPES IN FILO CUPS

JELLIED TOMATO SALAD

1½ sachets of powdered gelatine
850 ml/1½ pt natural tomato juice
salt and freshly ground black
pepper
2 cloves garlic, peeled and
crushed
6 spring onions, trimmed and finely
chopped
8 black olives, stoned and finely
chopped
2 large firm tomatoes, wiped (or
skinned if preferred) and finely
chopped
2 bunches of watercress, washed
and picked over

1 Dissolve the gelatine in 150 ml/5 fl
oz of the tomato juice (see page
21). Return to the rest of the tomato
juice and season to taste with salt
and pepper.
2 Stir in the crushed garlic.
3 Dampen six small moulds (I use
metal ring moulds) and divide the
onions, olives and chopped tomato
between them. Pour over the
tomato-juice mixture and chill for at
least 6 hours to set.
4 Turn out on to chilled plates by
dipping the moulds into hot water,
and garnish with the watercress. If
you have used ring moulds, put the
watercress in the middle; otherwise,
put it to one side of the plate, or if
you have time, arrange it all the
way round the mould like a little
nest.

CHICKEN AND HERB RISOTTO

2 tbsp vegetable oil
1 large onion, peeled and chopped
2 cloves garlic, peeled and
crushed
425 g/15 oz arborio rice
2 litres/2½ pt home-make chicken
stock (see page 17)
meat from the boiling chicken used
for the stock, cut into small, bite-
sized pieces
salt and freshly ground black
pepper
3 tbsp chopped fresh herbs

1 Heat the oil in a large saucepan
and cook the onion over a medium
heat, stirring occasionally, until soft
and transparent – about 5 minutes.
Add the garlic and rice and
continue to cook over a medium
heat, stirring constantly, for 5
minutes – until the rice is well coated
with oil, and shiny.
2 Meanwhile, in another saucepan,
bring the stock to the boil. Ladle just
enough of the simmering stock into
the first saucepan to just cover the
rice. Keep cooking the rice over a
moderate heat, stirring constantly,
until all the liquid has been
absorbed. Ladle on more stock and
continue cooking until the rice is
done: this will take about 20–25
minutes. Add more stock as each
batch is absorbed. The finished
risotto should be quite wet and
creamy, but with a little 'bite' left in
the middle of each grain of rice. This
process might not use up all the
stock; on the other hand, it may all
be used up before the rice is done,
in which case continue adding ▷

notes

*Parsley will do if no other
fresh herbs are available. Basil
or tarragon would be
particularly good. Do not use
rosemary or sage: both are too
strongly flavoured and not good
to eat raw.*

◁ boiling water instead of stock.
3 About 2–3 minutes before the rice is cooked, stir in the chicken to heat through. Season if necessary with salt and pepper, but the stock will probably have seasoned the rice sufficiently.
4 Serve in hot soup plates, sprinkled with herbs. Do not sprinkle indiscriminately with Parmesan cheese: remember, this will add lots of extra calories and if you have used lots of nice fresh herbs, would be quite unnecessary anyway.

GRAPES IN FILO CUPS

6 sheets of filo pastry (the remainder of the packet can be frozen)
6 tbsp low-fat natural yoghurt or fromage blanc
550 g/1¼ lb seedless green or black grapes, washed and dried and separated (if you cannot get seedless grapes, then cut each grape in half and remove the seeds)

1 Heat the oven to 220°C/425°F/ Gas Mark 7.
2 Fold each sheet of filo in half and cut the folded sheet down to a 18-cm/7-in square. Repeat with the remaining sheets of pastry, so that you end up with twelve squares. Place one on another, turning it through 45 degrees, so that you end up with two layers and eight points. Repeat with the rest.
3 Lightly oil six individual ovenproof moulds on the outside. I use conical

metal dariole moulds, but they do not have to be metal – individual ceramic soufflé dishes would be fine. Place these upside down on a lightly oiled baking tray. Unless you have a very large oven and very large baking trays, use two trays with three moulds on each, or work in two batches.
4 Drop the double layers of pastry over the moulds, allowing them to take their own shape. Do not press them tightly up to the mould, or they will be difficult to remove when cooked.
5 Bake the pastry for about 2 minutes or until pale golden. Remove from the oven and turn the pastry and the mould upside down on the baking tray, so that the base is down, and the frill side up. Return to the oven for about another 2 minutes: do not allow them to get too dark. When done, remove from the oven and allow to cool. When they are cold, gently ease the pastry away from the moulds with a pointed knife, and the moulds will slip out easily, leaving crisp golden frilly pastry cases. Do be careful, though, as they are very fragile to handle: if you are nervous about damaging them, make a couple extra just in case.
6 Just before serving, place a spoonful of yoghurt in each pastry shell, and fill up with the grapes. Serve at once. (I think these are nicest with grapes, but you can, of course, use any fruit you like.)

notes

***Filo pastry** is bought ready made, usually frozen, from large supermarkets, Greek or Middle Eastern grocers, and delicatessens. These paper-thin sheets of pastry, made only from flour and water (with no added fat), are much used in Greek, Turkish and Middle Eastern cookery for sweet and savoury dishes. Keep all the pastry except the sheets you are working with at the moment covered with a damp cloth, as they are so thin that they quickly dry out, becoming brittle and difficult to handle.*

One of the greatest pleasures about holidaying in France is the food and I find it very difficult not to eat too much and become as fat as a pig at the end of a stay there. Luckily my favourite meal is not very fattening at all and whenever I see *assiette de fruits de mer* on a menu I almost always choose it. One of the best was also very inexpensive, particularly considering the quantity of oysters and other shellfish it contained. This was while staying overnight in a small one star hotel called 'Hotel de la Plage': not an unusual name, but this *plage* was in the pleasant Normandy seaside town of Saint-Jean-Le-Thomas.

MEAN

AND LEAN

menu 3

CREAM OF SWEDE SOUP

TURBAN OF FISH

HOT SALAD OF RICE AND WHEAT

ROSE PETAL CREAMS

CREAM OF SWEDE SOUP

1 large onion, peeled and chopped
450 g/1 lb swede, peeled and cut
into about 5-cm/2-in cubes
1.5 litres/2½ pt chicken stock (see
page 17) or vegetable stock
2 tbsp dried skimmed milk powder
salt and freshly ground black
pepper
chopped fresh parsley, dill,
tarragon, sorrel or chives as
available to garnish

1 Place the onion, swede and stock in a large lidded saucepan, bring to the boil, then turn down the heat and simmer, covered, for about 15 minutes, or until the swede is tender.
2 Liquidize the contents of the saucepan with the powdered milk. Return to the pan and reheat, adding salt and pepper to taste if needed.
3 Serve in heated bowls or dishes with a sprinkling of chopped herbs.

Valun is a small fishing port on the Yugoslavian island of Cres. Here we enjoyed fish eaten beside the sea it was caught in: perfect!

Alcohol is unfortunately fattening, containing large quantities of sugar. Sparkling mineral water makes a pleasant alternative to wine with a meal (dry white wine is the least fattening), but I so much enjoy a glass of wine with a meal that I 'diet' by making myself 'cheat' drinks to have before dinner. Mineral water with lots of ice, slices of lemon and fruit, perhaps some slices of cucumber or fresh mint – even flowers – looks such a treat that one hardly notices that it is non-alcoholic. A gin and tonic without the gin (slimline tonic, of course) is quite passable if you don't think about it too hard and a Bloody Mary tastes scarcely any different without the vodka if you add a good dash of Worcestershire sauce.

TURBAN OF FISH

675 g/1½ lb small plaice fillets
140 g/5 oz skinless whiting fillet or other inexpensive white fish like coley or silver pollack (which is very similar to cod, but much cheaper)
100 g/3 oz ricotta cheese
150 ml/5 fl oz fromage blanc or Quark
1 egg
2 tsp capers
1 tbsp chopped chives or spring onions
grated rind of ½ lemon
salt and freshly ground black pepper
a little vegetable oil

1 First skin the plaice fillets. This is very quick and easy if you have a good thin sharp knife. Place the fillet skin-side down on a chopping board. Hold the tip of the tail end with one hand, then slide the knife between the flesh and the skin as close to the tail as possible: if you use a sawing motion and keep the knife blade flat against the chopping board, the skin will quickly pull away from the fish. (A friendly fishmonger may do this for you if he is not busy.)
2 Heat the oven to 160°C/325°F/ Gas Mark 3.
3 Put the other white fish in the bowl of a liquidizer or food processor with the cheeses and the egg, and process until quite smooth. Add the capers, chopped chives or spring onions, the grated lemon rind and salt and pepper to taste, and process briefly – just long enough to

mix in the new ingredients, but not long enough to chop the capers and the chives/spring onions too finely.
4 Lightly oil a 1.1-litre/2-pt ring mould and line it with the plaice fillets, putting the side which once had the skin attached uppermost – that is, the other side against the mould. Do this as neatly as possible, but if there are one or two small gaps, it doesn't matter. These should be some bits of fish left protruding above the top of the mould.
5 Fill the mould with the purée and level the top with a knife. Now fold over the protruding bits of plaice on to the purée and flatten off as much as possible. This whole process takes an awful lot of words to describe, but is in fact very quick and simple indeed.
6 Cover the mould with kitchen foil, then bake in a bain-marie in the preheated oven for about 45 minutes, or until the filling is set.
7 Turn out on to a plate, being careful not to loose any of the juices that will come out with the 'turban'.
8 Bring to the table whole, perhaps with the centre filled with a fresh green vegetable like peas or beans, before serving in slices, moistened with the juice. Serve with the Hot Salad of Rice and Wheat.

HOT SALAD OF RICE AND WHEAT

**250 g/8 oz wholewheat grains
(available from wholefood stores)
225 g/8 oz basmati or other long-
grain white rice**
The dressing
**4 tbsp low-fat natural yoghurt
1 clove garlic, peeled and crushed
juice of ½ lemon
1 tbsp chopped chives or spring
onions
1 tbsp finely chopped parsley
salt and freshly ground black
pepper**

1 Place the wholewheat grains in a
medium saucepan half-full of
boiling water and simmer, covered,
over a low heat for 1 hour.
2 About 20 minutes before the
wheat is cooked, boil the rice by
your favourite method, or
according to the instructions on the
packet.
3 Meanwhile make the dressing by
mixing the yoghurt with the garlic,
lemon juice, chopped chives or
spring onions and parsley, and
season to taste with salt and
pepper.
4 Drain the rice and the wheat when
they are both cooked, and mix
together in a heated bowl or
serving dish with the yoghurt
mixture. Serve immediately. Any
leftovers are good cold.

ROSE PETAL CREAMS

**150 ml/15 fl oz cold water
1 tbsp sugar (or the equivalent of
non-fattening sweetener)
1 sachet of powdered gelatine
1 tbsp powdered skimmed milk
575 ml/1 pt skimmed milk
1 tbsp triple distilled rose water
(available from good chemists)
pink food colouring (optional)
a handful of sweetly scented pink
or white rose petals (the old-
fashioned kind is best)**

1 Put the water and sugar in a small
saucepan, sprinkle over the
gelatine and dissolve (see
page 21).
2 Dissolve the milk powder in the
skimmed milk and pour into a bowl
or large jug. Mix in the gelatine/
syrup mixture. Mix in the rose water.
You can colour the mixture very
faintly with a few drops of pink
colouring: if you object to adding
any colour, then omit it and use
white rose petals. It will look very
pretty, but somehow it tastes more
of roses if it is pink.
3 Pour into six small glasses or
bowls, or one large bowl, and chill
until set – at least 4 hours. This is not
meant to set as stiffly as a jelly, so
do not attempt to turn it out.
4 When the cream is set, scatter
with rose petals just before serving.
The petals can be eaten, so don't
overdo them: two or three per
person is quite enough. If you don't
want to eat the petals, you don't
have to – just put them to one side.

This is a lovely delicately
*flavoured dessert to be made
when roses are in season. It is
really simply a milk jelly and
can be flavoured with other
things at other times of the
year: vanilla, almond, etc.
If you are not trying to lose
weight, it is richer if made with
full cream milk, and quite
sumptuous if you flood the top
with a little thin cream before
floating on the rose petals.*

notes

MEAN

AND LEAN

menu 4

FENNEL SOUP
WITH KIPPER 'CROÛTONS'

PASTA WITH SCORCHED PEPPERS,
COTTAGE CHEESE AND
SPRING ONIONS

DRIED FRUIT AND APPLE JELLY

Pasta seems almost inextricably linked with Bolognese sauce outside its home country, and yet this and other meat sauces are seldom offered on menus in restaurants in Italy: most are based on fish, cheese and vegetables. The classic dishes are always the most popular, though each cook has his own individual recipe. Even simple sauces like pesto will taste quite different in different restaurants; 'Tunu' in the Ligurian village of Dolcedo was no exception. A friend suggested that they expand into the large courtyard behind, so what was once an unprepossessing concrete yard is now a picturesque dining terrace with apricot cloths, some extraordinary Art Nouveau sideboards covered in scarlet geraniums and, through a wall of plants in terracotta pots, tantalizing glimpses of sky, hills covered in olive trees and crumbling Renaissance towers. Here again we lunched well and cheaply on spaghetti with pesto, osso bucco with peas, cheese and fruit. Kittens chased each other over the gravel under our feet while cheeky sparrows flew close over our heads looking for crumbs.

notes

Garlic *is obtainable now all year round. Look for fat, juicy bulbs. Like parsley it is universally popular as a flavouring, though as the most strongly flavoured member of the onion family its pungent and delicious flavour should be used with discretion.*

FENNEL SOUP WITH KIPPER 'CROÛTONS'

1.75 litres/3 pt chicken stock (see page 17) or vegetable stock
450 g/1 lb bulb fennel (weighed after trimming), trimmed and roughly chopped (save any sprouting feather tops and chop them finely to garnish the soup)
2 cloves garlic, peeled and crushed
2 tbsp powdered skimmed milk
salt and freshly ground black pepper
115–170 g/4–6 oz boneless kipper fillet

1 Place the stock and fennel with the garlic in a large saucepan, bring to the boil, turn down the heat and simmer, covered, for about 20 minutes, or until the fennel is soft.
2 Liquidize the contents of the saucepan with the skimmed milk powder and season to taste with salt and pepper.
3 Meanwhile, remove the skin from the kipper fillets in the same way as for the plaice in the Turban of Fish (page 104) and cut the flesh into small cubes, measuring about 5 mm/½ in thick, and place in a small bowl. Pour over boiling water, leave for 5 minutes and drain: the kipper will then be cooked.
4 Serve the soup in heated bowls or dishes and divide the kipper 'croûtons' between them. Sprinkle with any reserved chopped green fennel tops.

PASTA WITH SCORCHED PEPPERS, COTTAGE CHEESE AND SPRING ONIONS

2 medium red peppers
2 medium green peppers
2 medium yellow peppers
500 g/18 oz dried pasta (any shape you fancy) or 700 g/24 oz fresh
4 large or 6 small spring onions, trimmed and chopped
350 g/12 oz low-fat cottage cheese
salt and freshly ground black pepper

1 Cut the peppers into flat strips and discard the seeds. Place in batches on kitchen foil under a hot grill, skin-side up, and leave until the skin is completely blackened. This will take about 5–10 minutes, depending on the peppers and the heat of your grill. Place in a plastic bag and leave for 5 minutes. The skins will then easily be removed under a running cold tap. Drain, roughly chop and reserve.
2 Cook the pasta in plenty of salted boiling water, for the time it says on the packet if using the dried kind, or for about 2–3 minutes if using fresh.
3 Drain the pasta and tip into a large heated serving bowl, with the chopped onions, the cottage cheese and the chopped peppers. Mix all together well and season to taste with salt and pepper.
4 Serve immediately in heated soup dishes or bowls.

DRIED FRUIT AND APPLE JELLY

1 sachet of powdered gelatine
575 fl oz/1 pt white grape juice
2 medium apples (red-skinned look nicest)
115 g/4 oz mixed dried fruit (currants, raisins, sultanas)
6 tbsp low-fat natural yoghurt

1 Dissolve the gelatine in 75 ml/3 fl oz of the grape juice (see page 21) and then mix the gelatine mixture with the rest of the grape juice.
2 At the last minute (to prevent discolouration), core (but do not peel) the apples. Chop into quite small pieces about 5 mm/¼ in square and mix with the dried fruit. Divide this between six small moulds (if you wish to turn out the jellies) or six small glasses. Pour over the gelatine/fruit juice mixture, dividing it equally, and chill until set – at least 6 hours.
3 If using moulds, turn out on to chilled plates by dipping the moulds into hot water and place 1 tbsp of yoghurt beside each little jelly. If using glasses, place the yoghurt on top of the jelly in the glass.

If you cannot find all three colours of pepper for the pasta recipe, make up the quantity with whatever you can get. Red and green peppers are usually easily available for most of the year. Although they will look very unattractive when you take them from under the grill, once they are skinned their jewel-like colours will be revealed, and the flesh will be sweet and succulent.

notes

MEAN

AND LEAN

menu 5

GRAPEFRUIT AND SHELLFISH SALAD
SERVED IN TWO SHELLS

STUFFED SQUID

LETTUCE PARCELS
WITH PURÉED PEAS

FROMAGE BLANC
WITH FRUIT PURÉES

The menu at 'The Wharf' restaurant on Pier 4 in Walsh Bay, Sydney, Australia, takes full advantage of the excellent local fresh fish. One memorable meal there began with tiny deep purple octopus cooked with sun-dried tomatoes until perfectly soft and tender, smothered with curling chives and surrounded by a salad of miniature vegetables, and 'tweed head bugs', an extraordinary local shellfish that looks quite prehistoric but which tastes delicious.

Home-cooked shellfish are, of course, the best, but frozen make good substitutes. Beware when buying cockles or mussels cooked, shelled and loose from a fishmonger that they have not been soaked in vinegar, which would overpower the flavours of everything else. Fishmongers will often sell you scallop shells for next to nothing. If you are a regular customer, they may even give them away. The concave half-shell makes the better container.

Pine kernels are the seeds of the Mediterranean stone pine. They can be eaten raw or roasted and salted as a snack. Use sparingly in soups, stews, rice dishes and confectionery, as they are an expensive luxury. Delicatessens and specialist food shops sell them in small packets, but I find it cheaper to buy them loose from a wholefood shop. Use chopped mixed nuts in the squid recipe if you cannot get them.

GRAPEFRUIT AND SHELLFISH SALAD SERVED IN TWO SHELLS

115 g/4 oz cooked shelled prawns (thawed if frozen)
115 g/4 oz cooked shelled mussels
115 g/4 oz cooked shelled cockles
3 large grapefruit
1 tbsp capers, drained and chopped
6 large radishes (or 12 small ones), trimmed, wiped and thinly sliced
salt and freshly ground black pepper
1 box mustard and cress, cut from its box, or shredded lettuce
6 scallop shells, scrubbed and dried, to serve

1 Mix together all the shellfish in a medium-sized bowl.
2 Cut the grapefruits in half and remove the flesh with a sharp knife. (If you have a specially made grapefruit knife which has a curved, serrated blade, this makes the task much quicker.) Perform this task over the bowl containing the shellfish, so that none of the juice is wasted. Reserve the empty shells. Cut the flesh into bite-sized pieces and add to the shellfish.
3 Add the capers and the sliced radishes and season to taste with salt and pepper. Pile the mixture into the empty grapefruit shells.
4 Place each one on a scallop shell and garnish with mustard and cress or shredded lettuce.
5 Serve chilled or at room temperature, depending on the weather and season.

STUFFED SQUID

about 1 kg/2¼ lb medium-sized squid (thawed if frozen), cleaned (see page 73)
1 tbsp olive oil
1 medium onion, peeled and chopped
225 g/8 oz cooked white rice
45 g/1½ oz currants
45 g/1½ oz pine kernels
1 tbsp chopped parsley
grated rind of 1 lemon
1 clove garlic, peeled and crushed
salt and freshly ground black pepper
350 ml/12 fl oz vegetable or fish stock
2 tbsp concentrated tomato purée

1 Heat the oven to 160°C/325°F/ Gas Mark 3.
2 If you have cleaned the squid yourself you will have the tentacles. Chop these very finely.
3 Heat the oil in a small saucepan and cook the onion (with the chopped tentacles, if you have them) over a medium heat for about 5 minutes or until the onion has softened and looks transparent.
4 Tip the contents of the pan into a bowl and add the rice, currants, pine kernels, parsley, lemon rind and garlic. Mix well and season to taste.
5 Stuff the squid tubes loosely with the rice mixture and either sew up the open ends with thread or secure with a wooden cocktail stick.
6 Arrange the stuffed squid in one layer in an ovenproof dish.
7 Heat the stock in a small saucepan and stir in the tomato purée until dissolved. (If there is any

of the stuffing mixture left over, stir this in too.) When it is almost boiling, pour over the squid and cover the dish with its lid or with kitchen foil. Cook in the centre of the preheated oven for 1½ hours.
8 Remove the thread or skewers.
9 The stuffed squid can be served whole, but look much better sliced on to hot plates. Surround with the sauce they were cooked in and serve with Lettuce Parcels with Puréed Peas, a green vegetable, or a simple salad.

LETTUCE PARCELS WITH PURÉED PEAS

350 g/12 oz peas (frozen are fine)
1 tbsp fromage blanc or Quark
salt and freshly ground black pepper
6 large cos lettuce leaves or Chinese leaves
vegetable oil

1 Cook the peas in boiling water until tender.
2 Drain the peas and purée in a food processor or liquidizer with the fromage blanc or Quark and season to taste with salt and pepper.
3 Meanwhile, blanch the lettuce leaves in boiling water for 3–4 minutes or until wilted. Drain and refresh in cold water. Drain again and pat dry on clean tea towels or kitchen paper.
4 If the thick stem near the base is still quite stiff, trim this flat with the leaf, using a sharp knife, so that the whole leaf is pliable.

5 Place one sixth of the pea purée in the centre of each leaf. Fold over first the stalk end, then the sides, and roll over to form a neat parcel.
6 Arrange these little parcels, seam-side down, in one layer on one large or two small lightly oiled plates (depending on what will fit comfortably into your steamer).
7 Steam over boiling water for about 10 minutes, or until heated through, and serve immediately.

FROMAGE BLANC WITH FRUIT PURÉES

125 g/4½ oz dried apricots
225 g/8 oz fresh strawberries or other soft fruit (thawed if frozen)
6 heaped tbsp fromage blanc or Quark

1 To make the apricot purée, soak the dried apricots according to the instructions on the packet (the ones marked 'quick soak' or 'no soak' need only about 2 hours). Drain and cook in just enough water to cover in a small saucepan, covered, over a medium heat. Cook until they are tender and all the liquid has been absorbed: this should take about 15 minutes, but keep an eye on the pan near the end of cooking time. Do not let it burn. Cool and purée in a food processor or liquidizer.
2 Purée the strawberries or other fruit and chill both purées.
3 To serve, divide the cheese and each of the fruit purées between six chilled plates.

notes

Fromage blanc is a soft fresh French cheese which is now widely available. The percentage of the fat content is usually marked on the container, so if you are trying to lose weight buy the carton marked '0 per cent fat'. Quark is a similar low-fat soft fresh cheese from Germany.

Cuisine Nouvelles Pauvres

TO BE SERVED FRESH strawberries and cream is always a treat, but to be offered a beautiful little case of mouth-watering home-made sweet pastry filled with prettily arranged strawberry halves enclosing a pyramid of whipped cream – looking as if it might have come from the most exclusive Parisian pâtisserie – is even more so. The tarts certainly take considerably longer to prepare, but this will be a pleasure for those who enjoy cooking and the finished results – and the compliments – will be reward enough. The tarts will not only earn you praise from your appreciative guests, but will also cost you very little to produce. That is what this chapter is about: creating very special meals, pampering your guests, and showing off a little – and why not?

For a really special meal, presentation is particularly important, and it is here that we can learn from the great nouvelle cuisine chefs of France. The recipes of these highly acclaimed culinary originators are, more often than not, way beyond the skills and budgets of most home cooks. Great chefs usually have unlimited funds and large numbers of staff under them, necessary for elaborate last minute presentations of the dishes. For them it is nothing to garnish with a few out-of-season crayfish or slices of fresh truffle. We will have only one pair of hands (with perhaps another pair at the last minute if we're lucky) for our final presentation, and crayfish and truffles will be way beyond our means. What we can do, however, is to use a little more time and patience to create our own very special dishes. We can take time to wrap little vegetable parcels in leaves or mix our own mayonnaise. We can also take just a little longer with the final presentation of each dish and pinch an idea or two from those great chefs of France.

As often as possible, arrange the food on each plate rather than bringing it to the table in serving dishes. That way your meal will look just how you want it to, and you won't end up with messy-looking half-empty serving dishes cluttering up the centre of your table. This is all much easier if you don't have to eat in the kitchen. A cold first course can be put in place on the table just before the guests arrive. With hot dishes, it is best to get someone else to quietly pop out and help you at the last minute, if you can. That way you can serve a spectacular-looking meal without being away from your guests for more than a few minutes. No special meal is a treat for the guests if the cook is away somewhere for ages slaving in the kitchen. After all, when entertaining friends, the food is only a part of the enjoyment.

To make an occasion special, not only should your delicious food look attractive on the plates, but the table should look good too. This need not cost a lot: a personal and original touch or a dramatic flourish is better than any amount of money spent. A cluster of ten cheap white household candles blazing in the centre of an all-white table setting has far more impact than two expensive tapered pastel-coloured ones. A huge bowl crammed with a mass of bright yellow dandelions is much more effective than a few tastefully arranged expensive florist's flowers.

Plates need not be matching, or even new. Odd ones can be found with no trouble in junk shops and jumble sales for next to nothing. Collect plates of the same size and stick to a colour theme – all white, or all blue and white, in different patterns, perhaps. Apart from the fun of searching, you will soon acquire an attractive collection. Good old-fashioned heavy cutlery is also not difficult to find in bits and pieces, and cleans up well; a collection of odd pretty glasses will be more pleasing than a set of modern machine-made ones. All these oddments provide conversation pieces and an original touch of your own, making the perfect setting for your very special meals.

CUISINE

NOUVELLES

PAUVRES

menu 1

MARBLE TEA EGGS
WITH ORIENTAL MAYONNAISE

MANDARIN CHICKEN LIVERS IN
GOLDEN BOXES

SPICED PANCAKES WITH GREEN
GINGER SAUCE

MARBLE TEA EGGS WITH ORIENTAL MAYONNAISE

9 hard-boiled eggs
about 1.1 litres/2 pt strong
Indian tea
2 tbsp dark soy sauce
The oriental mayonnaise
1 egg
150 ml/¼ pt vegetable oil
2.5-cm/1-in cube fresh ginger,
peeled and crushed
1 clove garlic, peeled and crushed
dash of soy sauce
juice of ½ a small lemon
¼ tsp sugar
salt
pinch of chilli powder
To serve
½ cucumber, very thinly sliced
1 carton of mustard and cress
paprika

1 Crack the shells of the hard-boiled eggs all over but do not remove them. Place in a saucepan with enough tea to cover. Add the soy sauce, bring to the boil and simmer for 1 hour. Cool, then shell and halve the eggs.
2 To make the mayonnaise, place the raw egg in a liquidizer and with the motor running, pour on the oil slowly. Add the ginger, garlic, soy sauce, lemon juice and sugar and blend thoroughly. Season with salt to taste and chilli powder.
3 To serve, cut the cucumber rounds into squares and arrange in a V shape on each plate. Make a bed of mustard and cress at the open end of each 'V' and arrange 3 egg halves on top. Spoon a little mayonnaise over the eggs and dust with paprika.

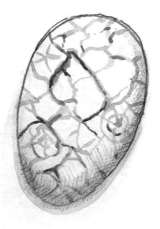

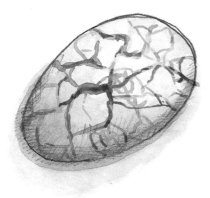

notes

If you have *a liquidizer or food processor it is almost as quick to make your own mayonnaise as it is to open a jar. This method, which uses a whole egg rather than just the yolk, is almost foolproof. I have made it hundreds of times and the only one occasion when mine curdled (I had to nip out and buy a jar) was when the weather was very thundery. This is what you do.*
Put 2 eggs with 2 tsp salt, 1 tsp dry English mustard and a good grind of black pepper (white is better as it doesn't leave dark specks) in a food processor or liquidizer. Turn on the motor and slowly pour in 300 ml/10 fl oz oil (I use half vegetable oil and half olive oil, but you can use less olive oil if you wish, or even all vegetable oil). In a few seconds you will have lots of beautiful thick mayonnaise. Blend in the juice of half a lemon, and check the seasoning.

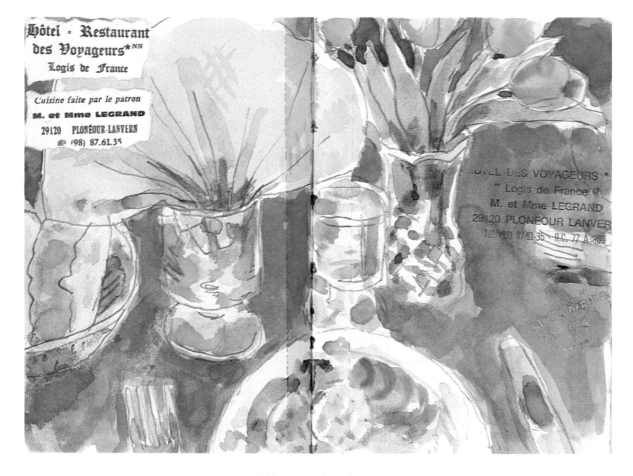

Table settings do not have to be elaborate or expensive to be effective. In this pleasant French restaurant simple flowers and a colourful cloth made a memorable setting for an equally memorable meal.

MANDARIN CHICKEN LIVERS IN GOLDEN BOXES

1 quantity of home-made puff
pastry (see page 63)
1 egg yolk, beaten with 1 tbsp milk
50 g/2 oz butter
1 small onion, peeled and chopped
1 clove garlic, peeled and crushed
450 g/1 lb chicken livers, washed,
trimmed and diced
250 ml/8 fl oz fresh orange juice
3 mandarins, peeled and
segmented
salt and freshly ground black
pepper
450 g/1 lb cabbage, steamed and
buttered

1 Heat the oven to 220°C/425°F/
Gas Mark 7.
2 Roll out the pastry to a 5-mm/¼ in
thickness and cut six 10 cm/4-in
squares. Brush the tops with the egg
and milk glaze. Using a sharp knife,
lightly score a lattice pattern on the
top of each square. Place the pastry
squares on a damp baking sheet
and bake in the preheated oven for
15 minutes or until golden. Remove
from the oven, slice off the tops and
set aside. Remove any uncooked
dough from the pastry bases and
keep them warm.
3 To make the filling, heat the butter
in a frying pan and cook the onion
and garlic over a medium heat until
transparent. Add the chicken livers
and cook, stirring continuously, until
the blood stops running (this will
take about 3–4 minutes). Lift the
livers out of the pan with a slotted
spoon and keep warm. Add the
orange juice to the pan and allow

to bubble for 2–3 minutes, then add
the fruit and season to taste. Return
the livers to the sauce and allow to
bubble gently for 1 minute.
4 Have ready six warmed dinner
plates and divide the cabbage
between them. Place a pastry box
on each plate and spoon in the
chicken liver mixture. Cover with the
reserved lids and serve at once.

SPICED PANCAKES WITH GREEN GINGER SAUCE

115 g/4 oz plain flour
2 eggs
¼ tsp salt
300 ml/½ pt milk
1 tsp mixed spice
oil for frying
150 ml/¼ pt green ginger wine
1 heaped tsp arrowroot dissolved
in 1 tbsp water
1 × 200-g/7-oz can blackcurrants
in natural juice, drained

1 Mix together the flour, eggs, salt,
milk and mixed spice to make a
smooth batter, and allow to rest for
30 minutes to 1 hour.
2 Heat a medium frying pan, brush
with a little oil and make six
pancakes. Keep warm.
3 To make the sauce, heat the
ginger wine in a small saucepan
with the dissolved arrowroot. When
it has thickened, add the
blackcurrants and warm through.
4 Cut each pancake from the centre
to the edge. Place one on each of
six warmed plates and pinch in
even pleats to form a fan. Spoon
over a little of the hot sauce.

Mandarins are sometimes
hard to find, although they are
usually available around
Christmas time. If you cannot
obtain them use clementines,
satsumas or small oranges
instead. Clementines and
satsumas are especially good
because they contain almost no
pips at all. If you do use
oranges remember to remove
any pips from the segments
with the point of a sharp knife
before adding the fruit to the
filling.

notes

C U I S I N E

N O U V E L L E S

P A U V R E S

menu 2

TWO-FISH TERRINE

*HOT SHELLFISH SALAD
IN PANCAKE BASKETS*

LITTLE STRAWBERRY TARTS

TWO-FISH TERRINE

1 bay leaf
1 tsp salt
½ tsp whole black peppercorns
a strip of finely peeled lemon rind
juice of ½ lemon
small bunch of parsley or parsley stalks
1 spring onion, trimmed and roughly chopped, or 1 thick slice of a medium onion
450 g/1 lb fillet of plaice (or other white fish), skinned
170 g/6 oz fillet of trout, skinned
2 tsp ready-made pesto sauce
1 quantity of mayonnaise (see page 117)

1 Pour enough water into a medium-sized deep frying pan or sauté pan to come halfway up the sides. Add the bay leaf, salt, peppercorns, lemon rind and juice, parsley and onion. Bring to the boil and simmer, covered, over a low heat for 15 minutes. Strain through a fine sieve. Discard the solids and return the liquid to the same pan.
2 Meanwhile, line a lightly oiled 850 ml/1½ pt loaf tin with kitchen film.
3 Poach half the plaice or other white fish fillets in the liquid over a low heat for about 2 minutes only: do not overcook, as the fish will continue to cook in the mould from its own heat. Drain and pat dry with kitchen paper. Pack the fish into the lined tin as evenly and neatly as possible, placing the fish fillets lengthways in the tin, trimming off any uneven bits and using the trimmings to fill in any gaps.
4 Working as quickly as possible, repeat the process with first the trout and then the remainder of the white fish. You should then have two layers of white fish sandwiching a layer of pink trout.
5 Cover the top with more kitchen film and then place a heavy flat weight on top to press the terrine as it cools. You can cut a piece of stiff card to shape and place some heavy cans or other weights on top, or use another similar loaf tin filled with weights.
6 Leave to cool and press for about 12 hours or overnight.
7 Mix the pesto with the mayonnaise.
8 Just before serving turn out the terrine, remove the kitchen film and cut into six thick slices (or six thinner ones, leaving the rest for lunch next day).
9 Arrange a slice on each plate with a little spoonful of pesto mayonnaise on either side.

In general I usually buy the big flat open field mushrooms, as they have the most flavour, but they do add a greyish colour to pale sauces, so in this recipe I think it is best to use the small white button mushrooms.

These pancake baskets are easy and fun to make as well as tasting good. They are also very versatile and can be used as containers for all kinds of fillings – hot or cold, sweet or savoury. They make an interesting change from pastry cases.

HOT SHELLFISH SALAD IN PANCAKE BASKETS

100 g/3½ oz plain flour
2 eggs, lightly beaten
200 ml/7 fl oz milk
1 tsp melted butter
a pinch of salt
50 g/2 oz butter
3 spring onions, trimmed and chopped
170 g/6 oz mushrooms, sliced
2 cloves garlic, peeled and crushed
grated rind of ½ lemon
1 tbsp chopped parsley
300 ml/10 fl oz double cream
salt and freshly ground black pepper
115 g/4 oz fresh shelled prawns
115 g/4 oz shelled cockles
225 g/8 oz shelled mussels

1 Make a smooth batter with the flour, eggs, milk, butter and salt. Heat the oven to 180°C/350°F/Gas Mark 4.
2 Lightly oil a medium-sized frying pan and heat over a medium heat. Make six pancakes in the usual way, using about 2–3 tbsp of the mixture for each one, and cooking them until golden brown on each side. Stack them as they are cooked on a plate.
3 Lightly oil the outside of six ovenproof moulds and place on a lightly oiled baking tray.
4 Place a pancake over each mould, arranging them evenly into 'flutes', and bake in the centre of the preheated oven for 15–20 minutes, or until they are crisp. Remove from the oven and allow to cool. Leave

the baskets on the moulds until you need them.
5 For the salad, heat the butter in a medium pan over a medium heat and cook the onion and mushroom for about 5 minutes, stirring occasionally. Add the garlic, lemon rind, parsley and cream and season to taste with salt and pepper. Bring to the boil and simmer over a low heat for 2–3 minutes. Add all the shellfish and cook for 1 minute more, just to heat them through. Do not overcook, or they will toughen.
6 Meanwhile, remove the little pancake baskets from their moulds and put them, open-side up, back on the baking tray. Reheat for 2–3 minutes in a preheated oven at 220°C/425°F/Gas Mark 7.
7 Place each pancake basket on a warmed plate and fill with some of the shellfish mixture. Serve with green vegetables or a simple salad.

LITTLE STRAWBERRY TARTS

225 g/8 oz plain flour
pinch of salt
2 tbsp icing sugar
115 g/4 oz unsalted butter, chilled
1 egg, lightly beaten
1 scant tbsp chilled water
300 ml/10 fl oz double cream, whipped until stiff
225 g/8 oz small strawberries, hulled and halved
3 black grapes

1 In a medium bowl, mix the flour, with the salt and sugar and rub in the butter until the mixture

resembles fine breadcrumbs. Mix in the egg and water and bring together to form a smooth dough. Chill in a plastic bag for 1 hour.
2 Roll out the pastry and line 6 large individual flan tins (loose bottomed ones are the best). Press a piece of kitchen foil into each one and fill with some beans or rice (to stop the pastry puffing up).
3 Bake on baking sheet in a preheated oven at 200°C/425°F/ Gas Mark 7 for about 15 minutes. Remove the beans/rice and foil and continue to cook for about 5 minutes more or until the pastry is crisp and brown. Cool and remove

the pastry cases from the tins.
4 Fill a piping bag with a large nozzle with the cream and fill each pastry case with cream, piping it up into a conical shape.
5 Press the strawberry halves into the cream, all the way round each tart, pointed sides up, cut side out and sloping in towards the top. Place a halved grape rounded side up on the top of each tart.
6 Arrange on pretty plates to bring to the table. If you have a cake stand, so much the better. I have a pretty Victorian one in rose pink which looks lovely with these strawberry tarts.

As a travel writer I am occasionally lucky enough to spend some time in rather special hotels like the 'Villa Sant' Andrea' in Taormina in Sicily. Originally the beachside residence of an English family, the hotel retains much of the charm of the old house and reminders of the tastes of its former occupants, with antique furniture and odd bookshelves in corners full of old and rather dusty English books.

menu 3

SCARBOROUGH FAIR PANCAKES

*PARMESAN SOUFFLÉS IN FISHY
BASKETS*

*CRUMBED APPLES WITH ORANGE
AND CRANBERRY SAUCE*

SCARBOROUGH FAIR PANCAKES

225 g/8 oz plain flour
2 heaped tsp baking powder
1 tsp salt
freshly ground black pepper
225 ml/9 fl oz milk
2 eggs
2 tbsp chopped fresh parsley
1 tsp chopped fresh sage
1 tsp chopped fresh rosemary
1 tsp chopped fresh thyme
oil for frying
To serve
1 small jar of cocktail gherkins,
thinly sliced lengthways
150 ml/¼ pt soured cream, or
thick Greek-style yoghurt
6 tsp clear honey

1 Mix together the flour, baking
powder, salt, pepper, milk and
eggs to form a smooth batter. (This
is easily done in a food processor.)
Stir in the parsley, sage, rosemary
and thyme.
2 Drop tablespoons of the batter on
to a lightly oiled frying pan and
cook over a medium heat for 3–4
minutes, turning once, or until
cooked through and golden brown
on each side. Make eighteen
pancakes in all, working in
manageable batches and keeping
them warm in a covered dish in a
low oven.
3 Have ready six warmed dinner
plates. Place three pancakes on
each plate and arrange the gherkin
slices between them. Spoon a little
soured cream or yoghurt in the
centre of each plate and drizzle
over the honey.

PARMESAN SOUFFLÉS IN FISHY BASKETS

2 long leeks
6 small whiting fillets, skinned
salt
freshly ground black pepper
2 eggs, separated
2 tbsp double cream
50 g/2 oz freshly grated Parmesan
cheese
225 g/8 oz carrots, scrubbed,
thinly sliced and cut into diamonds
225 g/8 oz stick beans, cut into
2.5-cm/1-in lengths
225 g/8 oz broccoli, stalks cut into
thin rounds
225 g/8 oz petits pois, thawed if
frozen
225 g/8 oz red pepper, deseeded
and diced
1 clove garlic, crushed
115 g/4 oz butter, melted

1 Heat the oven to 220°C/425°F/
Gas Mark 7.
2 Remove 6 large outer leaves from
the leeks. Quarter the inner parts
lengthways, cut into 2.5-cm/1-in
sticks and reserve. Blanch the outer
leaves for 4 minutes, drain, pat dry
and reserve.
3 Season each fish fillet with the salt
and pepper and coil into a ring.
Fold the leek leaves in half
lengthways and wrap one around
the outside of each ring of fish.
Secure with cocktail sticks and
surround with strips of kitchen foil.
Place on a buttered baking sheet.
4 Mix the egg yolks with the cream
and Parmesan. Beat the egg whites
until stiff and gently fold into the
egg-yolk mixture. Spoon a sixth of
the soufflé mixture into the centre ▷

*If you do not have fresh herbs
and use dried ones instead,
halve the quantities. Either
way, make sure you chop the
herbs really finely. This recipe
is really much nicer made with
fresh ones, though, and you
will be able to enjoy their
wonderful smell of the
countryside.*

Little gadgets for removing the cores from apples, pears and other fruit can be bought quite cheaply from most good hardware shops and kitchen departments. They save a lot of time and bother, performing their task efficiently and neatly in seconds.

To finish a meal with champagne or a dessert wine is a real treat, but both are very expensive. Try serving a good-quality sweet cider with this or any other apple dessert. Make sure it is really cold.

◁ of each leek-wrapped fish ring and cook in the preheated oven for 15–20 minutes, until the soufflés are well risen and golden brown.

5 Meanwhile, steam the carrots, beans, broccoli, peas and red pepper with the reserved sticks of leek until just cooked. Stir the crushed garlic into the melted butter and toss the vegetables in the garlic butter. Season to taste.

6 Have ready six warmed dinner plates. Remove the foil from the soufflé-filled fish rings and place one in the centre of each plate. Surround with the steamed vegetables.

CRUMBED APPLES WITH ORANGE AND CRANBERRY SAUCE

225 g/8 oz fresh white breadcrumbs
1 tbsp white sugar
½ tsp ground cinnamon
3 small apples, peeled, cored and very thinly sliced into rings
plain flour
2 eggs, beaten
115 g/4 oz butter
The sauce
200 ml/7 fl oz fresh orange juice
1½ tsp arrowroot dissolved in a little water
1 × 175-g/6½-oz jar cranberry sauce

1 Mix together the breadcrumbs, sugar and cinnamon. Dip the apple rings first in flour, then in beaten egg, then in the breadcrumb mixture.

2 Gently heat the butter in a frying pan and fry the apple rings in batches over a medium heat until crisp and golden. Keep warm.

3 To make the sauce: in a small saucepan, heat the orange juice with the arrowroot and cranberry

'ARDECHOISES' VINEYARDS + HILLS

sauce, stirring continuously until the sauce thickens.

4 Have ready six warmed plates. Pour a little sauce on to each, top with a circle of overlapping apple rings and drizzle a little more sauce on top.

I invented the recipe for Scarborough Fair Pancakes while camping in the Ardèche. The ingredients were close at hand – and free! The sky is a brilliant blue, but not the same raw turquoise which it is near the coast: it is softer, almost as if it had absorbed a little colour from the lavendor which covers the hillside fields in long cushioned stripes. Colours are altogether more gentle here than in coastal Provence, except, that is, for the occasional fields ablaze with smiling sunflowers, whose great yellow heads turn towards us (or is it to the sun?) as we drive past on narrow dusty roads to Saturday market. The early morning air is fresh and sparkling and the sun, already hot and bright, dapples through the leaves of the plane trees which form graceful avenues on straight stretches of the road. The warm scents of wild herbs, sage, rosemary and thyme, blown in through the open windows of the car, are exhilarating, and sharpen our appetites for *grands cafés crèmes* and croissants in Uzès.

CUISINE
NOUVELLES
PAUVRES

menu 4

ASPARAGUS EN CROÛTE

KIDNEYS IN RED CABBAGE PARCELS

SWEET POTATO CAKES

BLACK FOREST BLANCMANGE

ASPARAGUS EN CROÛTE

12 medium-sized asparagus spears, trimmed (frozen would just do in an emergency, in which case I would add 1 clove crushed garlic to the cream cheese)
about ⅔ quantity of home-made puff pastry (see page 63)
115 g/4 oz cream cheese, softened
salt and freshly ground black pepper
1 egg yolk mixed with a little milk
2 bunches of watercress, washed and picked over and well drained
1 quantity of vinaigrette (see page 29), with garlic if you like

1 Cook the asparagus in a pan of boiling salted water for about 5–10 minutes or until just tender. Do not overcook. Drain and pat dry on kitchen paper. Allow to cool. (If using frozen, cook for a little less time than it says on the packet.)
2 Roll out the pastry thinly and cut six rectangles measuring about 20 × 11.5 cm/8 × 4½ in. Heat the oven to 220°C/425°F/Gas Mark 7.
3 Spread a sixth of the cream cheese (with the garlic mixed in, if using frozen asparagus) down one half of each pastry rectangle, but not going right to the edge: leave a border of about 1 cm/½ in.
4 Season the cheese with a little salt and pepper and arrange two cooked asparagus spears on top, trimming them if they are too long. Reserve the trimmings.
5 Brush the pastry border lightly with water and fold over the pastry to enclose the filling, pressing the dampened edges together to seal.

Brush the top of each parcel with the egg glaze.
6 Arrange the parcels on a dampened baking sheet and cook in the centre of the preheated oven for about 20 minutes, or until the pastry is crisp, golden and risen.
7 Meanwhile, toss the watercress in the dressing. Chop any asparagus trimmings and add these to the salad. Arrange the salad on six large plates.
8 When the parcels are cooked, place these in the centre of each salad and serve at once.

KIDNEYS IN RED CABBAGE PARCELS

1 large red cabbage
50 g/2 oz butter
675 g/1½ lb lambs' kidneys (weighed after trimming), trimmed of any hard bits, and cut into bite-sized pieces
1 small onion, peeled and chopped
salt and freshly ground black pepper
½ tsp dried sage (or 1 tsp fresh if available)
½ tbsp flour
2 tsp dry English mustard
½ tbsp redcurrant jelly
50 ml/2 fl oz red wine (if you haven't any opened, use white – or ordinary tea)
300 ml/10 fl oz chicken, vegetable or beef stock
85 g/3 oz mushrooms, wiped and sliced

1 Cook the cabbage whole in a large saucepan of simmering ▷

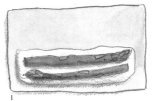

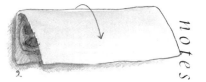

notes

This delicious early summer vegetable has a very short season and an asparagus bed takes many years to get established. Unless you are lucky enough to grow your own asparagus will remain an expensive luxury. Hot with melted butter and lemon juice or hollandaise sauce, or cold with mayonnaise, asparagus makes the perfect summer starter. This is an unusual and economical way of serving this lovely vegetable, making a little go a long way.

notes

The red cabbage in this recipe not only gives its own very distinct taste, but looks spectacular. However, if you are in a hurry, you could use a white or green cabbage: the leaves separate much more easily. If you use the red kind, you will be left with quite a lot of part-cooked cabbage. Use this as a vegetable the next day: stew it slowly with a good knob of butter, a finely chopped onion and lots of pepper, in a covered pan over a low heat, for about 30 minutes. If you have a cooking apple handy, this added with onion makes it even tastier.

◁ salted water, covered, for 30 minutes. Drain and cool.

2 Very carefully remove 6 large leaves. This is a fiddly job, as you will find, but be patient – I think the finished result and the compliments make it well worth the effort. The odd hole or small tear around the edges doesn't matter as these will be folded in, so long as the centre of each leaf remains intact.

3 Boil these leaves for another 10 minutes until quite tender. Drain, cool and pat dry on kitchen paper. If the stems at the base end remain a little stiff and unbendable, trim them level with the leaves, using a sharp knife.

4 Meanwhile, melt half the butter in a medium saucepan and cook the kidneys over a medium heat, stirring constantly, for 2–3 minutes. Do not overcook, or they will toughen. Remove from the pan with a slotted spoon and place in a bowl or dish. Reserve. Preheat the oven to 190°C/ 375°F/Gas Mark 5.

5 Add the onion to the pan and season to taste with salt and pepper and the sage. Cook over a medium heat, stirring occasionally, for 5 minutes or until well softened. Remove with a slotted spoon and mix in with the kidneys.

6 Add the remainder of the butter to the pan and melt, then add the flour and cook, stirring constantly, for 2 minutes; then add the mustard, redcurrant jelly, wine and stock. Bring to the boil simmer, stirring constantly, until thickened – about 2–3 minutes. Add the sliced mushrooms and continue to cook for 3 minutes more.

7 Add to the sauce any juices which

have by now drained from the kidneys and onions and collected in the bottom of the bowl or dish. Divide the kidney mixture between the six leaves and make neat parcels (see the diagram for making the Lettuce Parcels with Puréed Peas on page 113).

8 Arrange these parcels in one layer, seam-side down, in a shallow ovenproof dish, pour over the sauce and cover the dish with its lid or kitchen foil. Cook in the centre of the preheated oven for 30 minutes.

9 Arrange the parcels on heated plates and pour over the sauce. Serve with the Sweet Potato Cakes and another vegetable if you are feeding very hungry people, but it isn't really necessary.

SWEET POTATO CAKES

550 g/1¼ lb sweet potatoes
25 g/1 oz melted butter
1 egg, lightly beaten
115 g/4 oz plain flour
1 tsp baking powder
½ tsp salt
freshly ground black pepper
vegetable oil for frying

1 Heat the oven to 220°C/425°F/ Gas Mark 7. Bake the sweet potatoes in their skins until quite soft. The time will depend on the size of the potatoes. They take a little less time than ordinary potatoes, but will need about 30 minutes to 1 hour. When cooked, allow to cool, remove the flesh and discard the skins. Mash the flesh well with a potato masher or fork. You should have about 450 g/1 lb.

2 Mix in the butter and egg. Mix the flour with the baking powder and salt and pepper to taste. Mix the dry ingredients into the potato mixture with a fork.

3 With floured hands gather the mixture together and lift it on to a floured work surface. Knead lightly to form a soft scone-like dough. Roll out with a floured rolling pin to 1 cm/½-in thickness and cut into 12 shapes with a 5-cm/2-in round pastry cutter, or a small glass.

4 Fry in a lightly oiled frying pan over a very low heat for 15 minutes, turning once, or until cooked through and browned on both sides. Work in two batches if necessary.

BLACK FOREST BLANCMANGE

1 sachet of powdered gelatine
150 ml/5 fl oz water
115 g/4 oz plain chocolate, broken into pieces
150 ml/5 fl oz milk
300 ml/10 fl oz double cream
1 x 284-g/10-oz can of black cherries in natural juice, drained and pitted
3 tbsp (or miniature bottle) brandy (*not optional*)

1 In a medium saucepan dissolve the gelatine in the water (see page 21) and pour into a jug. In the same pan dissolve the chocolate in the milk over a low heat, stirring occasionally. Add the chocolate mixture to the gelatine mixture with half the cream and stir well. Pour into six small wetted moulds or one 600-ml/1-pt mould and chill until set – at least 6 hours, or up to 24.

2 Meanwhile, put the cherries in a small bowl with the brandy, cover tightly with kitchen film and leave to macerate.

3 Turn out the blancmanges by dipping the mould in hot water. Serve with the macerated cherries and the remaining cream.

A cherry stoner is another relatively cheap and invaluable little kitchen gadget to be found in most good kitchen supply stores or departments. I use mine more often for stoning olives.

notes

CUISINE
NOUVELLES
PAUVRES

menu 5

BLINIS WITH THREE FILLINGS

RIBBONS OF LIVER
WITH BLACK CHERRY SAUCE
AND DEEP-FRIED CABBAGE

RASPBERRY FOOL

BLINIS WITH THREE FILLINGS

The blinis
225 g/8 oz plain flour
2 heaped tsp baking powder
1 tsp salt
freshly ground black pepper
275 ml/9 fl oz milk
2 eggs
vegetable oil for frying
The fillings
115 g/4 oz taramasalata, bought ready prepared
150 ml/5 fl oz thick Greek-style yoghurt
small jar of black lumpfish roe
50 g/2 oz cream cheese, softened
115 g/4 oz shelled prawns (thawed if frozen)
6 parsley leaves or sprigs (depending on whether you are using the Continental flat-leaved type or the ordinary one)

1 Mix together the flour, baking powder, salt, pepper to taste, milk and eggs to form a smooth batter
2 Drop tablespoons of the batter on to a lightly oiled frying pan and cook over a medium heat for 3–4 minutes, turning once, or until cooked through and golden brown on each side. Make eighteen pancakes in all, working in manageable batches and keeping them warm in a covered dish in a low oven.
3 Just before serving, and working quickly to keep the blinis warm – if you get someone to help you it will only take a few seconds – spread the taramasalata on six pancakes. Divide the yoghurt between six more and top with spoonfuls of lumpfish roe. Spread the remainder with the cream cheese and pile the prawns on top of these. Put a parsley leaf or sprig in the centre of the taramasalata-filled ones.
4 Place one of each kind on each of six warmed plates. Serve at once.

Blinis are really Russian pancakes served with lots of different toppings. Mine are 'cheat' ones, as they are leavened with baking powder instead of the traditional yeast, but they take much less time to make and are, I think, just as nice.

Real caviar is the roe of the sturgeon, and prohibitively expensive. Salmon roe is cheaper and delicious but still a real luxury item. Lumpfish roe, which is easily available in little pots, makes an adequate and tasty substitute. It is a very good starter served just on its own with toast, lemon wedges and black pepper. Buy it in red or black varieties: both are better if you rinse them thoroughly first, otherwise they tend to 'bleed' on to other foods.

notes

Arrowroot is a nutritious starch made from the powdered roots of various tropical plants. It is quite tasteless, and a liquid thickened with arrowroot will retain an almost transparent appearance. It can be bought in most supermarkets, grocers and also chemists.

Many Chinese restaurants offer a delicious deep-fried 'seaweed' among the starters on their menu. This is in fact often just deep-fried cabbage which, as you will see in this recipe, is very easy to make.

RIBBONS OF LIVER WITH BLACK CHERRY SAUCE AND DEEP-FRIED CABBAGE

The sauce
1 x 284-g/10-oz can of black cherries in natural juice, pitted
juice and finely grated rind of 1 orange
juice of 1 lemon
finely grated rind of ½ lemon
1 heaped tbsp redcurrant jelly
good dash of Worcestershire sauce
1 heaped tbsp arrowroot
You will also need
675 g/1½ lb lambs' liver, trimmed and cut into 1-cm/½-in 'ribbons'
seasoned flour
oil for frying
675 g/1½ lb green cabbage (spring greens are ideal), washed and dried thoroughly and cut into the narrowest strips possible
oil for deep frying
6 lemon wedges

1 First make the sauce. Put the cherries with the juice from the can with the orange and lemon juice and rind, the redcurrant jelly and the Worcestershire sauce in a medium saucepan. Heat over a low heat, stirring occasionally, until the jelly has melted. Mix the arrowroot with a little water and stir this into the sauce. Continue to heat, stirring constantly, until the sauce comes to the boil and thickens. It should not be too thick, but if you think it is too thin, add a little more arrowroot. Reserve and keep hot.
2 Toss the liver strips in the seasoned flour and shake off any excess. Heat a little oil in a large frying pan and cook the liver strips over a medium heat, stirring constantly, for 3–4 minutes or until just cooked. Do not overcook, or the liver will become dry and tough. Cook in two batches if necessary. Keep warm in a covered dish in a low oven.
3 Fry the cabbage in very hot deep fat in batches for a few seconds, or until crisp. Drain well on crumpled kitchen paper, and keep warm in a low oven while you cook the rest.
4 Divide the liver 'ribbons' between six hot plates and spoon over some of the sauce. Serve with the fried cabbage and a lemon wedge to squeeze over it. Accompany with a very simple green side salad.

RASPBERRY FOOL

250 g/8½ oz raspberries (thawed if frozen)
300 ml/10 fl oz double cream, whipped till stiff
mint or lemon balm leaves

1 Liquidize the raspberries, reserving six perfect berries.
2 Fold the puréed fruit into the cream: it doesn't matter if you don't do this too thoroughly – in fact, I think it looks nicer with a slightly marbled effect.
3 Pile into six pretty glasses or dishes. Place one of the reserved raspberries on the top of each and decorate with the leaves.
4 Chill for at least 2 hours before serving.

An occasional visit to a more expensive restaurant provides me with food for thought as well as the stomach. The setting of this prettily decorated restaurant in Avignon heightened the enjoyment of superb food beautifully presented, and inspired me to new ideas of my own.

CHAPTER 6

Loaves and Fishes

SOME PEOPLE LIKE PARTIES and some people don't. I love them, and I enjoy giving parties almost more than I love going to them. For the last few years I have given a large one for between seventy and eighty people nearly every year. I have learnt that with careful advance planning, efficient organization on the day, and a little last-minute delegation, it is almost easier to entertain in this way than to give a small formal dinner party.

The amount of extra work and expense are the two things which tend to put off most people giving a 'proper' party. Neither of these need be a problem even when inviting a big crowd. Don't be overambitious and plan more than you will be able to cope with easily. One or two simple dishes are quite enough when catering for large numbers, and when the food is really delicious nobody expects a choice, although it is a good idea to check if any of your guests are vegetarian or have other reasons for not eating certain foods, and provide an alternative for them. If you give people too much choice, it is alarming how even the most normally restrained guests can turn into greedy monsters, helping themselves to enormous portions of everything at the same time, so that your carefully prepared food becomes a revolting mixture of tastes piled into a hideous mountain on somebody's plate.

When you announce that you are planning to have a party and friends offer to help, take them up on it – but be specific. The quality of 'my Nan's special trifle' can vary enormously! If someone whom you know makes terrible pastry offers to bring quiches, simply suggest that no-one in the world makes a better plain green salad than they do! Even someone who can't cook at all can bring some good bread or superlative cheese. An even better idea for a large party is to share it with a friend. Not only do you tend to get a more interesting guest list but you will be halving the work, cost and responsibility.

When people ask what to wear, don't just say, 'Oh, anything you feel comfortable in', or they will dress down. Everyone loves an excuse to get dressed up, and then they will arrive expecting a glamorous occasion and looking the part. Fancy-dress parties can be wonderful fun: often the quietest people, the ones who protest that they hate dressing up, will come in the most fabulous costumes.

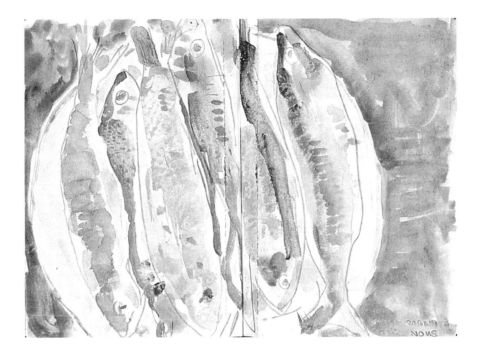

If all your friends are dressed in their best finery, I think it is a shame to expect them to eat off paper plates and drink from plastic cups. Borrow plates and cutlery from friends; and wine shops often lend glasses for nothing, or a small hire charge.

It would not be practical to hold large parties very often, but instead of having two dinner parties for six what I now do quite regularly is to hold one large dinner party for twelve people all sitting down together, making it a much more special occasion. I am lucky because I recently acquired a dining table which will seat twelve, but before that I managed perfectly well with a strong folding decorator's table, which looked just as good under a cloth.

Unless you are rich and can afford to supply all the drinks for your party, I think it is a good idea to ask guests to bring a bottle with them. I once had some formal-looking invitations printed for a large fancy dress party (the theme was 'Inhabitants of the Forest') and after 'Supper will be served at ten o'clock' it read 'Please bring rather more wine than you think you will drink'!

All the menus in this chapter will feed twelve people, but the quantities can easily be halved if you want to feed six, or expanded to feed more.

LOAVES
AND FISHES

menu 1

*CHILLED LETTUCE
AND PEA SOUP*

ROBIN'S SALMON CIRCLE

*PEAR TARTS WITH ALMOND
CUSTARD*

CHILLED LETTUCE AND PEA SOUP

2 large onions, peeled and finely chopped
2 large lettuces (cos are best) together weighing about 450 g/ 1 lb, washed, trimmed and roughly chopped
2.25 litres/4 pt chicken stock or vegetable stock (see page 17)
550 g/1¼ lb frozen peas
575 ml/1 pt milk
salt and freshly ground black pepper
chopped fresh mint, chives or parsley to garnish

1 Place the onions and lettuces in a large saucepan with the stock and bring to the boil. Turn down the heat and simmer, covered, for 10 minutes. You can split the quantities and use two saucepans if you do not have one big enough: I use a preserving pan with kitchen foil for a lid.
2 Add the peas and continue to simmer gently for 5 minutes after the liquid returns to the boil.
3 Liquidize in batches and return to the pan with the milk. Reheat and season to taste with salt and pepper.
4 Chill very thoroughly – overnight is best – and serve in chilled bowls or dishes with a sprinkling of chopped herbs.

ROBIN'S SALMON CIRCLE

1 large onion, peeled and finely chopped
225 g/8 oz butter
2 × 439-g/15½-oz cans of salmon
225 g/8 oz breadcrumbs, preferably wholemeal
6 eggs, lightly whisked
grated rind of 2 lemons
salt and freshly ground black pepper
vegetable oil and flour, for preparing moulds
The sauce
5 tbsp liquid from salmon (made up with vegetable oil if not enough)
2 tbsp cornflour
850 ml/1½ pt milk
juice of 2 lemons
salt and freshly ground black pepper

1 Cook the onion in 25 g/1 oz of the butter in a small saucepan over a medium heat until soft and transparent. Melt the remaining butter in another pan (do not let it brown), reserve and allow to cool. Heat the oven to 180°C/350°F/ Gas Mark 4.
2 Drain the salmon, reserving the liquid, and place the fish in a bowl, mashing with a fork to break up the flakes. Add the onion, breadcrumbs, eggs, lemon rind and melted butter. Mix all together well and season to taste with salt and pepper – not too much salt, as the salmon may already have a lot.
3 Lightly oil two 1-litre/2-pt ring moulds, dust with flour to coat and tip out any excess. (If you do not ▷

This recipe was given to me by a dear Australian friend who cooked it whilst staying with us. It is very quick, cheap, simple and surprisingly delicious. Robin insisted it be made with red salmon, but pink would do and I have also had excellent results with tuna. I have yet to try it with leftover cold fresh salmon: I have such greedy friends, there never are any leftovers!

◁   have ring moulds, use other
ovenproof moulds or loaf tins.)
4 Divide the mixture between the
two moulds, smoothing the tops.
Cover the moulds tightly with foil
and either bake in a bain-marie in
the preheated oven, or steam over
boiling water, for 1 hour.
5 Meanwhile, make the sauce.
Strain the salmon liquid and mix
with the cornflour in a small bowl.
Pour the milk into a medium
saucepan and mix in the cornflour
mixture.
6 Bring to the boil, turn down the
heat and simmer gently, stirring
occasionally, for 2–3 minutes or
until thickened. Add the lemon juice
and season to taste.
7 Turn out the moulds on to serving
dishes and serve surrounded by
plain boiled potatoes with lots of
chopped parsley. Fill the middle of
the moulds with a green vegetable
like broad beans, broccoli or
courgettes, or – for a lighter meal –
a Watercress Salad (see page 44).
Hand the sauce separately.

notes

*The almond skins add extra
flavour to the custard;
however, if you prefer a
custard which is perfectly pale
and smooth, buy almonds
without their skins. I use the
ones with skins on and add the
faintest hint of yellow food
colouring to enhance the
appearance. For a vanilla
custard, simply use 600 ml/1
pt of cows' milk instead of the
almond 'milk' mixture and
flavour with a vanilla pod,
vanilla sugar or a few drops of
good-quality vanilla essence.*

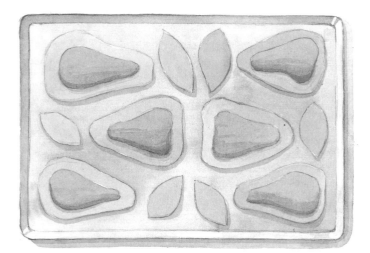

PEAR TARTS WITH ALMOND CUSTARD

2.25 litres/4 pt water
4 tbsp sugar
**2 tsp vanilla essence, or a vanilla
pod if you have one**
**6 large firm pears, peeled and
cored**
**1 quantity of home-made puff
pastry (see page 63)**
2 egg yolks, mixed with a little milk
**450 g/1 lb whole almonds with
skins**
600 ml/1 pt water
about 600 ml/1 pt milk
4 egg yolks
2 tbsp cornflour (slightly heaped)
2 tbsp sugar
**3 or 4 drops almond essence
(optional)**

1 In a large lidded saucepan put the
water, sugar and the vanilla
essence or vanilla pod. Bring to the
boil, turn down the heat and
simmer, covered, for 15 minutes.
Remove the vanilla pod (if you have
used one) at this stage, and dry it,
as you will be able to use it again.
2 Put the pears in the saucepan,
standing them upright in the syrup,
and cook, covered, over a medium
heat until quite tender. Do not worry
if the tops of the pears stick up out
of the water – the pointed ends do
not need so much cooking, and will
cook in the steam. The time will vary
very much according to the type of
pears, but will probably be
something between 30 minutes and
an hour; however, really hard pears
might take anything up to 1½
hours, so allow enough time
just in case.

3 When they are done, remove from the pan, drain, cool, and cut in half lengthways. Discard half the syrup, and boil the remainder over a fierce heat to reduce to 5–6 tbsp. Cool and reserve.

4 While the pears are cooking, heat the oven to 220°C/425°F/Gas Mark 7 and make the custard. Place the almonds and water in the bowl of a food processor or liquidizer and blend until the nuts have completely disappeared. Strain this liquid through a fine-meshed sieve into a measuring jug and make up to 1.1 litre/2 pt with milk. Discard the solids left in the sieve – unless you can think of something to do with them!

5 Bring this liquid to almost boiling point in a medium saucepan. Meanwhile, whisk the egg yolks with the cornflour and sugar until smooth and pale. Add the almond essence if used. When the milk is almost boiling, pour in a steady stream on to the egg-yolk mixture, stirring all the time. (I do this in seconds in my food processor.)

6 Strain through a sieve back into a clean saucepan and cook over the lowest heat possible until thickened. The custard will not go lumpy if stirred all the time and never allowed to come to the boil. Taste the custard and if you find the flavour too subtle, add 3–4 drops of almond essence – but be careful not to overdo it, or your beautiful home-made custard will end up with a synthetic taste. Cover the pan and reserve. The custard is nice hot or cold with this dish. If you decide to serve it hot, reheat it just before serving.

7 Roll out the pastry thinly and lay the drained pear halves, cut-side down, on top. Cut around each pear so that there is a border of pastry, measuring about 1 cm/½ in, following the shape of the pear. Arrange the pears on the pastry on a dampened baking sheet. Cut some leaf shapes from the pastry scraps and arrange these in the spaces left on the baking tray. Brush the tops of the pastry border and the 'leaves' with the egg glaze, being careful not to let it run over the edges of the pastry (this seals the layers when cooking and prevents the pastry from rising as well as it should). Bake in the centre of the preheated oven for about 20 minutes, or until the pastry is crisp, golden and well risen.

8 Remove the 'tarts' from the oven and brush the pears with the reserved syrup.

9 Arrange the cooked 'tarts' on hot plates with a little custard and decorate with pastry leaves, putting them at the thin end of the pear shape to look as if they are growing from the stem.

I like to have a selection of tablecloths so I can ring the changes with my table settings. White damask needs a lot of laundering but always looks wonderful (look for second-hand ones: even if they will not wash really white, they can be dyed to great effect). New tablecloths and napkins are often surprisingly expensive, but any washable material will make cloths, and a cheap remnant of some attractive fabric can quickly have its edges neatened on a sewing machine to provide expensive-looking table linen. All sorts of things can make attractive table coverings, from bedspreads to straw matting – use your imagination!

notes

LOAVES
AND FISHES

menu 2

VEGETABLE TERRINE

LAMBS' LIVER IN BRIOCHE

CHESTNUT AND GINGER
SOUFFLÉ

VEGETABLE TERRINE

115 g/4 oz vine leaves, or blanched lettuce leaves
225 g/8 oz carrots
225 g/8 oz long green French beans (the round kind, not 'runner')
675 g/1½ lb ricotta cheese
3 eggs, lightly beaten
170 g/6 oz cooked ham, finely chopped
1½ tsp dry English mustard
salt and freshly ground black pepper
1 large ripe avocado
2 quantities of mayonnaise (see page 117), with 2 crushed garlic cloves mixed In

1 Drain the vine leaves. Soak in hot water for 30 minutes, then drain and pat dry on kitchen paper.
2 Line the bottom and sides of a lightly oiled 850 ml/1½ pt loaf tin, reserving enough leaves for the top. Preheat the oven to 180°C/350°F/ Gas Mark 4.
3 Peel the carrots and cut into long narrow strips about 5 mm/¼ in across. Cook in boiling salted water for 5 minutes, refresh in cold water, drain and pat dry in kitchen paper.
4 Top and tail the beans and cook exactly as the carrots.
5 Mix the ricotta with the eggs, ham and mustard, and season to taste with salt and pepper. (I do this in my food processor: if you have not got one, the ham must first be chopped very finely.)
6 Put a thin smooth layer of this mixture in the bottom of the lined loaf tin using just less than a quarter

of the mixture. Now cover this with the beans, placing them in a neat, even layer lengthways in the tin.
7 Cover the beans using another quarter of the cheese mixture, then arrange the carrots on top and cover with another quarter of the cheese mixture.
8 Quickly peel and halve the avocado, remove the stone and cut into long thin slices. Working quickly so that the avocado does not have time to discolour, arrange the slices lengthways in the mould. Cover with the remainder of the cheese mixture.
9 Fold over any bits of vine leaves which are sticking up over the edge of the tin and use some more whole ones to cover the top of the cheese and vegetable filling completely.
10 Cover the mould tightly with kitchen foil and bake in a bain-marie in the preheated oven for one hour. Remove and leave to cool. Chill for at least 4 hours or overnight.
11 Unmould the terrine and cut into twelve even slices. Serve with a little of the garlic mayonnaise next to each slice.

notes

Vine leaves are obtainable in plastic packets, usually preserved in brine, from Greek and Turkish shops, delicatessens and specialist food shops. They need thoroughly rinsing and soaking in hot water for about 30 minutes before use. If you have access to fresh ones, of course use those (they just need blanching). Vine leaves are used extensively in Turkish, Greek and Middle Eastern cookery, and are most commonly associated with dolmades, where they are stuffed with rice and minced meats.

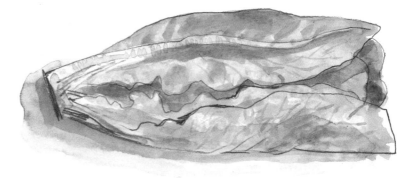

LAMBS' LIVER IN BRIOCHE

4 tbsp olive oil
2 large onions, peeled and chopped
1 tsp dried sage (or 2 tsp fresh)
2 pieces of lambs' liver each weighing about 550 g/1¼ lb
salt and freshly ground black pepper
1 egg, beaten, to glaze
The dough
675 g/1½ lb plain flour
1 tsp salt
3 tsp 'quick-action' yeast
2 tsp sugar
4 eggs
170 g/6 oz melted butter
4 tbsp hot water

1 Place 2 tbsp of the oil in a medium saucepan and cook the onions over a medium heat, stirring occasionally, until soft and transparent. Remove from the heat, mix in the sage and reserve.
2 Heat the remaining oil in a large frying pan and cook the two pieces of liver for 5 minutes each side, or until almost cooked through. Do not over cook as it will continue to cook in the oven.

3 Now make the dough: mix the flour, salt, yeast and sugar in a large bowl and then mix in the eggs, the melted butter and the water. Work together to form a soft dough and knead on a floured surface for 10 minutes. (This is easily done in a food processor.)
4 Divide the dough in two and roll each piece out to a rectangle just a little larger than the liver pieces and just over twice as wide. Place one liver piece down the centre of each piece of dough and, dividing the onions in two, place them on top of the liver. Season well with salt and pepper.
5 Bring up the sides of the dough, wrapping one slightly over the other, and dampening slightly with a little water to seal. Bring over the two ends so that the liver and onions are in a nice neat parcel. Drop each 'parcel', seam side down, into a lightly oiled 850-ml/1½-pt loaf tin and leave to rise somewhere warm until doubled in size: it will probably take about 2–3 hours in a warm kitchen – it is better if you do not hurry the rising process. Meanwhile, heat the oven to 220°C/425°F/Gas Mark 7.
6 Brush the top of each 'loaf' with egg glaze and bake in the preheated oven for about 30 minutes or until crisp and golden.
7 Turn the 'loaves' out and while still hot, cut each into six even slices. As the liver does not come right to the ends of the brioche, I cut a slice from each end first (these are delicious toasted for breakfast next day). Serve on warmed plates with a selection of fresh vegetables, simply cooked.

CHESTNUT AND GINGER SOUFFLÉ

The custard
575 ml/1 pt milk
2 egg yolks
1 heaped tbsp cornflour
1 tbsp sugar
½ tsp vanilla essence
You will also need
1 × 225-g/8-oz jar of Chinese stem ginger in syrup
1 × 435-g/15.3-oz can of unsweetened chestnut purée
grated rind of 1 orange
2 sachets of powdered gelatine
juice of 1 orange made up to 100 ml/4 fl oz with water
150 ml/5 fl oz double cream
2 egg whites
icing sugar (optional)

1 First make the custard. Bring the milk almost to boiling point in a saucepan. While this is heating, whisk the egg yolks with the cornflour, sugar and vanilla essence until pale. When the milk is almost boiling, pour it in a steady stream on to the egg mixture, whisking all the time (this is easiest in a food processor). Strain through a sieve back into the saucepan. Cook over the lowest possible heat until thickened. (This custard will not go lumpy if stirred all the time it is cooking.) Pour into a large bowl and leave to cool.
2 Pour all the syrup from the ginger jar on to the custard and mix this in well, with the chestnut purée and the orange rind (also easily done in a food processor).
3 Dissolve the gelatine in the orange juice and water mixture over

a low heat (see page 21) and mix into the chestnut mixture. Chill until just beginning to set.
4 Meanwhile, remove three pieces of the stem ginger, cut each evenly into four and reserve for garnishing. Chop the rest of the ginger finely.
5 Whip the cream until it is stiff. Whip the egg whites until they are stiff but not dry. Fold first the cream, then the egg whites and lastly the chopped ginger into the chestnut mixture.
6 Spoon the soufflé mixture into either one large dish or twelve small dishes or glasses. Chill until set – at least 4 hours, or overnight.
7 Just before serving you can dust the tops with a little icing sugar shaken through a fine sieve if you like, and then decorate with the pieces of reserved ginger.

Chestnut purée is available in cans, but be careful: some of it is already sweetened and flavoured with vanilla. This is more expensive, and would not be very successful in savoury dishes.

Chinese stem ginger in syrup is exactly what the name implies: whole pieces of ginger preserved in a sugar syrup. It is quite expensive (although prices vary enormously, depending on the brand name), but has a strong flavour and a little goes a long way – as in this recipe. Buy it loose from wholefood stores if you can – it will be much cheaper than the ginger sold in fancy packaging.

menu 3

'LONDON PARTICULAR'

LITTLE HAM
AND APRICOT TARTS

TRIPLE FRUIT TERRINE

CHARGING THE GRADOS

11·PM·

One of the best parties I have ever been to was a New Year's celebration in our hotel on a visit to Moscow. The meal started very late, after we returned from seeing the Moscow State Circus – a treat in itself – with an extremely varied hors d'oeuvre course which included lots of real caviar. After much jollity and fuelled with quantities of vodka and Russian champagne we braved the bitter cold to join the midnight crowds in Red Square.

When visiting London in winter foreign tourists are disappointed that they can no longer experience 'a foggy day in London town'. Until the 1960s, though, the inhabitants of the metropolis were frequently enveloped in the familiar dense, damp and choking greenish smogs nicknamed by Londoners 'pea soupers'. Dishes combining dried peas and ham have been popular in England since the Middle Ages. During Charles Dickens' time this comforting velvety soup often sustained the Victorian city dwellers against the damp miserable fog which Dickens christened 'a London Particular' in his book Bleak House. The name stuck and is now synonymous with both the fog and the soup.

'LONDON PARTICULAR'

2 tbsp vegetable oil
2 large onions, peeled and chopped
3 litres/5 pt ham stock (see page 24)
750 g/1 lb 10 oz 'quick-soak' peas, soaked according to instructions on the packet
freshly ground black pepper
Worcestershire sauce

1 Heat the oil in a medium saucepan and cook the onion over a medium heat, stirring occasionally, until soft and transparent.
2 Tip into a large saucepan. (You can split the quantities and use two saucepans if you do not have one big enough, or use a preserving pan covered with kitchen foil.) Pour on the stock. Drain the peas and add them to the pan. Bring to the boil and simmer, covered, for 15–20 minutes, or until the peas are tender.
3 Liquidize in batches and return to the pan. Reheat and season with pepper to taste and a good dash of Worcestershire sauce. You almost certainly will not need extra salt if you are using ham stock, which usually contains enough.

LITTLE HAM AND APRICOT TARTS

The pastry
450 g/1 lb plain flour
½ tsp salt
225 g/8 oz cold lard, cut into small pieces
150 ml/5 fl oz cold water
115 g/4 oz butter
The filling
2 medium onions, peeled and chopped
85 g/3 oz flour
850 ml/1½ pt milk
4 tsp dry English mustard
115 g/4 oz grated Gorgonzola, Stilton or other blue cheese
225 g/8 oz dried apricots, soaked according to the instructions on the packet, then drained and chopped
550 g/1¼ lb ham from stock recipe (see page 24), chopped
freshly ground black pepper

1 First make the pastry. Place the flour and salt in a mixing bowl and rub in the lard until the mixture resembles fine breadcrumbs. Mix in the water and, working quickly, bring together the mixture until it forms a smooth dough. Wrap in plastic wrap and chill for 30 minutes before rolling out. (This dough can be made in a food processor.)
2 Bake twelve pastry cases as in the recipe for Strawberry Tarts (see page 123) and reserve.
3 Melt the butter in a medium saucepan and cook the onion, stirring occasionally, over a medium heat until soft and transparent. Stir in the flour and cook for 2 minutes, stirring constantly.

4 Pour in the milk and bring to the boil, then simmer, stirring occasionally, over a low heat for 2–3 minutes, or until the sauce is thickened and the raw flour taste has gone.

5 Stir in the mustard, cheese, apricots and ham and continue to cook for 2–3 minutes more, or until the cheese has melted.

6 Season with pepper to taste. Add salt only if necessary, as the ham and cheese are both rather salty.

7 Put the pastry shells back in the oven, preheated to 220°C/425°F/ Gas Mark 7, for about 5 minutes to reheat, then fill with the ham mixture.

8 Serve with a variety of fresh vegetables.

TRIPLE FRUIT TERRINE

**115 g/4 oz dried apricots, soaked overnight or according to instructions on packet
juice of 1 large orange
575 ml/1 pt clear, still, white grape juice
8 level tsp powdered gelatine
350 ml/12 fl oz white wine
225 g/8 oz raspberries
500 ml/16 fl oz whipping or double cream, whisked until thick
fresh fruit to garnish**

1 Drain the apricots, reserving the liquid, and place them in a small pan with the orange juice and just enough of the soaking water to cover. Cover pan and simmer gently until all the liquid has been absorbed and the fruit is tender. Allow to cool.

2 Pour 300 ml/½ pt of the grape juice into a small pan and sprinkle on exactly half of the powdered gelatine. Leave for 3 minutes to swell, then dissolve over a low heat. Do not allow to boil. Add the gelatine mixture to the remainder of the grape juice and allow to cool. Pour this into two very lightly oiled 900 ml/1½ pt loaf tins and chill in the fridge till set.

3 Pour half the wine into a small pan and dissolve the remainder of the gelatine in this. Add to remaining wine and cool.

4 Liquidize the raspberries with half the wine and gelatine mixture. Sieve to remove any pips and fold in half the cream. Pour on to the set jelly; in both tins smooth the surface and chill until set.

5 Liquidize the apricots with the remaining wine and gelatine mixture and fold in the remaining cream. Pour over the raspberry mixture, in both tins smooth and chill until set (at least 5 hours in the fridge, or overnight) dip tin briefly in hot water and turn out on to a flat board. Cut into thick slices and serve on chilled plates. Decorate with pieces of fresh fruit.

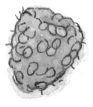

LOAVES
AND FISHES

menu 4

MIXED ANTIPASTI

CHOUX PUFFS OF PESTO CHICKEN
WITH MUSHROOMS

BROWNIE ORANGE MOUSSE

MIXED ANTIPASTI

1 quantity of 'Crudités' (see page 29)
1 quantity of 'Celery with Almond Cheese' (see page 71)
6 hard-boiled eggs, shelled and halved, or 36 hard-boiled quails' eggs, left in shells
a selection of raw and cooked vegetables, eg baby new potatoes, small courgettes, radishes, spring onions, etc, for dipping
1 quantity pesto mayonnaise (see page 121)
1 quantity garlic mayonnaise (see page 143)

1 Arrange all the ingredients except the mayonnaise on a large platter.
2 Put the mayonnaises in separate bowls and stand these either in the middle of the antipasti or on the table separately and allow the guests to serve themselves.

With a mixed hors d'oeuvre or antipasto you can be both imaginative and practical, transforming leftover meat, fish or vegetables into a delicious first course with some good flavoursome dressings. We ate a wonderful selection of hors d'oeuvres on a visit to the 'Au Bon Accueil', a small cosy restaurant in the heart of the French countryside.

notes

Pesto is a delicious sauce, found with small variations in many parts of the Mediterranean but mostly associated with Italy where it is served on hot pasta. It is made of fresh basil, garlic, pine kernels and either Parmesan or Sardo cheese pounded together with olive oil. It is often difficult to get hold of enough fresh basil to make this sauce at home unless you grow your own, but an excellent ready-made version is sold in little jars in Italian shops, delicatessens and large supermarkets.

CHOUX PUFFS OF PESTO CHICKEN WITH MUSHROOMS

The pastry
250 ml/8 fl oz water
115 g/4 oz butter
140 g/5 oz plain flour
1 tsp salt
4 eggs, lightly beaten
The filling
2 tbsp olive oil
2 medium onions, peeled and chopped
50 g/2 oz butter
225 g/8 oz button mushrooms, wiped and sliced
4 tbsp flour
850 ml/1½ pt chicken stock (see page 17)
675 g/1½ lb cooked chicken meat from the stock, with all fat and skin removed, cut into bite-sized pieces
3 heaped tsp ready-made pesto sauce
salt and freshly ground black pepper

1 Heat the oven to 200°C/400°F/ Gas Mark 6. Put the water in a medium saucepan with the butter, cut into small pieces, over a very low heat: the idea is for the butter to melt before the water boils to prevent evaporation affecting the quantities.
2 Sift the flour and salt on to a piece of greaseproof paper.
3 When the butter has melted, turn up the heat. As soon as the liquid boils, turn off the heat and slide all the flour and salt off the paper into the pan in one quick action.
4 Stir with a wooden spoon until combined, then turn the heat up

again to medium and stir the mixture over this until it forms a solid mass and comes away cleanly from the sides of the pan.
5 Remove the pan from the heat and allow to cool for 5 minutes.
6 Gradually beat in the eggs with a wooden spoon, and continue to beat until well mixed, glossy and smooth.
7 Make six even 'blobs' of the mixture on each of two dampened baking sheets. If you have a piping bag with a large nozzle, this is ideal; otherwise, just use a tablespoon. You will have twelve.
8 Bake in the preheated oven for 25 minutes, one above the other, switching them around halfway through the cooking time.
9 Remove the puffs from the oven and poke a little hole near the top of each with a sharp knife to allow the steam to escape. Return them to the oven for 5 more minutes. They should now be puffed right up and firm and golden on the outside with a dry hollow middle.
10 While the puffs are cooking, heat the oil in a medium saucepan and cook the onion over a medium heat, stirring occasionally, for about 5 minutes, or until soft and transparent.
11 Add the butter and when it has melted add the mushrooms and cook, stirring occasionally, for 2–3 minutes, or until just softened.
12 Add the flour and cook for 2–3 minutes more, stirring, then add the stock. Bring to the boil and simmer over a gentle heat, stirring occasionally. The sauce will thicken.
13 Add the chicken and continue to cook for 2–3 minutes more, just to

heat the meat through, then stir in the pesto sauce.

14 Check the seasoning and add salt and pepper if necessary.

15 Remove the puffs from the oven and slice a 'lid' off each. Place one puff base on each plate. Fill with chicken mixture, allowing it to overflow on to the plate. Replace the 'lids' and serve with colourful fresh vegetables such as broccoli and carrots.

BROWNIE ORANGE MOUSSE

The brownie
225 g/8 oz butter
225 g/8 oz sugar
2 eggs, well beaten
1 tsp vanilla essence
285 g/10 oz plain flour, sifted with
2 tsp baking powder
pinch of salt
3 rounded tbsp cocoa powder
juice of 2 oranges
The mousse
2 tbsp water
juice of 2 oranges
1 sachet of gelatine
575 ml/1 pt double cream
finely grated rind of 2 oranges

1 Heat the oven to 180°C/350°F/ Gas Mark 4. Meanwhile, melt the butter in a medium saucepan over a low heat: do not let it brown. Mix in the sugar and continue to cook, stirring constantly, for 2 minutes, then leave to cool for 3–4 minutes.

2 Add the eggs and vanilla, and then the flour, salt and cocoa. Mix well.

3 Spread the mixture evenly into two well greased baking tins measuring about 30 × 23 cm/12 × 9 in and bake in the preheated oven for 30 minutes. If you can't get the tins side by side on the shelf, put one above the other and swap round halfway through the cooking time.

4 When they are cooked, remove from the oven and while still hot, pour the orange juice evenly over the whole surface of the brownies. Leave to cool in the tins.

5 Mix the water and orange juice in a small saucepan, sprinkle over the gelatine and melt over a low heat.

6 Pour into a medium-sized mixing bowl and allow to cool. Add the cream and the orange rind and whisk until thick, but not too stiff.

7 Line two lightly oiled 850-ml/1½-pt loaf tins with kitchen film. Then, measuring very carefully, cut pieces from the brownie to fit first the bottom, then the sides, then the ends, and lastly the top. Only measure and cut one piece at a time so that you will not forget to allow for the thickness of the piece you have just put in. A few tiny gaps won't matter, but it should fit as well as possible.

8 Just before you put on the 'lids', fill each cake-lined tin with the orange mousse mixture. Smooth the top and gently but firmly press the lid into place (see diagram). Chill for at least 6 hours, or overnight.

9 Turn out the terrines, remove the kitchen film and cut into thick slices. Cut the end two slices from each terrine and give them to people with hearty appetites, as they will have cake on the ends as well as all the way round.

menu 5

*CURRIED PUMPKIN
AND ONION 'DAMPER'*

WATERCRESS SOUP

*CRUMBED BONED
CHICKEN WINGS*

GINGERED ORANGE CUSTARDS

notes

CURRIED PUMPKIN AND ONION 'DAMPER'

735 g/1 lb 10 oz peeled chopped pumpkin flesh (weight after peeling), steamed until tender
2 eggs, lightly beaten with 2 tbsp milk
550 g/1 lb 4 oz self-raising flour, sifted
about 2 level tsp curry powder (more or less as you like)
60 g/4½ oz butter
6 large spring onions, trimmed and chopped
salt and freshly ground black pepper

1 Mash the pumpkin with a potato masher, or purée in a food processor. Mix in the egg and milk mixture.

2 Put the flour and curry powder into a bowl and rub in the butter, as you would for making pastry. Mix the pumpkin mixture into this with the chopped onions and season to taste with salt and pepper. Turn out on to a floured work surface and knead lightly until smooth.
3 Divide the mixture in two and pat each in to a thick even round, the size of a medium frying pan. Score six wedges into the top of each with a sharp knife.
4 Oil two medium frying pans and cook the 'dampers' in these over a low-medium heat for 30 minutes, or until cooked through. Turn the dampers several times during the cooking period.
5 Serve with the following recipe (or any other soup), straight from the pan. It does not really need butter, but is certainly even more delicious with some.

This is a variation on a recipe from my beloved Australia, where such bread is cooked over a campfire in the outback. I once tasted something with the same name made by English Boy Scouts, which was a mixture of flour and water packed around the end of a stick and cooked in the flames of an open fire! I will draw a veil over this memory, and stick to the Aussie kind.

Chicken wings can often be found in 'bargain packs' for very little money indeed. They are wonderful for all kinds of things and are especially good barbecued. As they have lots of bones, they are normally best used as finger food. Boned and cooked this way, however, they not only make an easy-to-eat and elegant main course, but provide quantities of rich stock. This recipe can be prepared and crumbed in advance and then frozen if you like. I have cooked these chicken wings with great success for seventy people at a time.

WATERCRESS SOUP

4 bunches of watercress, washed and picked over
3.5 litres/6 pt chicken or vegetable stock
450 g/1 lb cooked potatoes
6 cloves garlic, peeled and crushed
salt and freshly ground black pepper

1 Pick off and reserve a few watercress leaves for garnish. Roughly chop the rest.
2 Put the chopped watercress in a large saucepan with the stock, potatoes and garlic. Bring to the boil and then turn down the heat and simmer, covered, for about 8 minutes.
3 Liquidize the contents of the pan, then reheat over a gentle heat and add salt and pepper if necessary.
4 Pour into heated soup bowls or dishes and float a few reserved watercress leaves on each serving.

CRUMBED BONED CHICKEN WINGS

2.3 kg/5 lb chicken wings
1 onion, quartered, but with the skin left on
1 carrot washed and cut in 4 pieces
2 sticks of celery
3 bay leaves
bunch of parsley or parsley stalks
a strip of finely peeled lemon rind
juice of ½ lemon
salt and freshly ground black pepper
The coating
seasoned flour
4 eggs, beaten (or more if needed)
285 g/10 oz stale white breadcrumbs
2 cloves garlic, peeled and crushed
115 g/4 oz melted butter
The sauce
3 oz butter
2 tbsp flour
850 ml/1½ pt chicken stock (from cooking wings)
juice of 2 lemons (or less if you don't want the sauce so lemony)
salt and freshly ground black pepper

1 Place the chicken wings in a large lidded saucepan with the onion, carrot, celery, bay leaves, parsley, lemon rind and juice, and season well with salt and pepper. Pour over water to cover by about 2.5 cm/1 in. Bring to the boil, then turn down the heat and simmer, covered, over a low heat for 1 hour.
2 Remove the cooked chicken wings from the pan. Strain the stock, discard the solids and reserve the liquid.

3 Now bone the chicken wings. This is a much easier job than it sounds, but you must work while the chicken is still hot: get someone to help if you can and the job will be done in no time.

4 First, using a sharp knife, cut off the narrow wing tip at the joint in the bones and discard. Now hold the remaining larger piece in one hand, gently but firmly. Find the end of the two little bones with the fingers of the other hand. Now with a little twist and a wriggle you will be able to slide out the bones, leaving a nice little torpedo-shaped pad of meat. Do not remove the skin. (Any that look a little messy can easily be patted back into a neat shape and will firm up and stick together when cold.) Leave to cool in one layer on a work surface.

5 Heat the oven to 220°C/425°F/ Gas Mark 7. Now dip each piece of chicken first in seasoned flour (shaking off the excess), then in egg, and lastly in breadcrumbs. Arrange them, as they are done, in a single layer on two lightly greased baking sheets.

6 Mix the crushed garlic into the melted butter and drizzle this evenly over the crumbed wings, making sure you miss none.

7 Bake in the preheated oven for 30 minutes or until piping hot, crisp and golden. If you have one tray above the other in the oven, swap them round halfway through the cooking time.

8 Meanwhile make the sauce. Melt the butter in a medium saucepan, add the flour and cook, stirring constantly, over a medium heat for 2–3 minutes. Add 710 ml/1¼ pt

chicken stock, bring to the boil, stirring constantly to make sure there are no lumps, then turn down the heat and allow to simmer for 5 minutes. Add the lemon juice and season with salt and pepper if necessary. Add more stock if the sauce is too thick. It should be quite light and runny.

9 Serve with either plain boiled rice or any of the other rice recipes in this book (double quantities), and simply dressed green salad. Hand the sauce separately.

GINGERED ORANGE CUSTARDS

6 eggs plus 2 yolks
juice of about 6 oranges
(500 ml/16 fl oz)
300 ml/10 fl oz double cream
300 g/11 oz sugar
2 tsp powdered ginger
icing sugar (for dusting)

1 Heat the oven to 180°C/350°F/ Gas Mark 4. Lightly grease twelve 8 cm/3 in ovenproof pots.

2 Whisk together all the ingredients (except the icing sugar) and pour into the pots.

3 Cover each with a small circle of greased kitchen foil and bake in a bain-marie in the preheated oven for 30 minutes or until the point of a knife inserted into the custard comes out clean.

4 Remove from the oven and allow to cool – the custards are best eaten warm, not hot. Dust with icing sugar before serving.

INDEX